Marx's *Capital*

Studies in Critical Social Sciences Book Series

Haymarket Books is proud to be working with Brill Academic Publishers (www.brill.nl) to republish the *Studies in Critical Social Sciences* book series in paperback editions. This peer-reviewed book series offers insights into our current reality by exploring the content and consequences of power relationships under capitalism, and by considering the spaces of opposition and resistance to these changes that have been defining our new age. Our full catalog of *SCSS* volumes can be viewed at https://www.haymarketbooks.org/series_collections/4-studies-in-critical-social-sciences.

Marx's *Capital*

Hegelian Sources

Andy Blunden

Haymarket Books
Chicago, IL

First published in 2025 by Brill Academic Publishers, The Netherlands

Published in paperback in 2026 by
Haymarket Books
P.O. Box 180165
Chicago, IL 60618
773-583-7884
www.haymarketbooks.org

ISBN: 979-8-88890-891-4

Distributed to the trade in the US through Consortium Book Sales and Distribution (www.cbsd.com) and internationally through Ingram Publisher Services International (www.ingramcontent.com).

This book was published with the generous support of Lannan Foundation, Wallace Action Fund, and the Marguerite Casey Foundation.

Cover design by Jamie Kerry and Ragina Johnson.

Printed in the United States.

Library of Congress Cataloging-in-Publication data is available.

Contents

Preface

In the companion volume to this work I have published a critique of the *Capital/Logic* debate. With this much more slender volume I present my own reading of how Marx used Hegel in his critique of political economy. Essentially, I show that the influence of Hegel is to be found in the *structure* of *Capital*, not in the similarity of some passages of *Capital* to some passages in Hegel's *Logic*.

The work is in three chapters. In the first chapter I briefly review the three sources and component parts (to shamelessly appropriate Lenin's phrase) of Marx's critique, namely Hegel's theory of science set out in the penultimate chapter of the *Logic*, Marx's use of history and Ricardo's political economy.

While I would have preferred to save the most challenging material till last, since the stimulus for writing the book was the need to show how Marx used Hegel's *Logic*, I cannot avoid dealing with the *Logic* in the very first section. If you are interested in the structure of Marx's *Capital* but not particularly interested in his debt to Hegel, you should still read this first section, but don't be put off if you find it arcane. The book gets easier to read with every section.

The first section also outlines Hegel's social theory which the reader will see is based on the coincidence of three moral realms. As will be seen, this structure reappears in Marx's *Capital*, though it is not the basis for the 3-volume structure of *Capital*, which nonetheless forms a transparently Hegelian syllogism.

The second section should be of interest to those who see *Capital* as a work of Logic for which the study of history is extraneous. On the contrary, Marx's use of history is essential to *Capital*. However, the way Marx uses history is distinctive and owes little to Hegel and indeed could be taken as a key element of Marx's critique of Hegel.

The third section on Marx's critique of the Political Economists also owes a debt to Hegel because here Marx follows Hegel's example in using the method of immanent critique which Hegel exhibited, for example, in the Introduction to the *Shorter Logic*.

The second chapter of this book is more or less a précis of the three volumes of *Capital*, chapter by chapter, although I skip over the last parts of Volume One and Volume Three of *Capital* and some chapters because they are not relevant to the development of the Hegelian structure of the argument. My précis is consistently focussed on tracing the structure of Marx's argument, and bringing out its Hegelian basis. In doing so I skim over material which may be important in other respects but otherwise blurs the main line of reasoning.

The third chapter of the book begins with a 3,000-word summary of the précis given in the second chapter, tracing the structure of Marx's argument in the most economical way possible. I summarise his argument three times over, each time illustrating one of three distinct levels of the structure of *Capital*. This brings out elements of the structure of *Capital*, which, so far as I know, no one has hitherto identified. Each of these structures is presented here for the first time.

After this, I review some issues which Marx has skipped over in his analysis of capitalism. The mode of production is indeed a fundamental determinant of the consciousness and activity of its denizens, and presents barriers to social change which are the most intractable. However, the development of the labour process which has unfolded, so far without bursting the confines of the capitalist mode of production, continues to transform our lives. Political, social, aesthetic and moral life are profoundly affected by the productive forces capitalism has unleashed irrespective of the form in which they are represented in capitalist society, namely as private property.

The capitalist mode of production makes societal infrastructure such as the internet and the other new forms of communication the private property of individual billionaires. It also places control of the destructive and dangerous impact of economic activity on the natural conditions of human life in the hands of a few capitalists and the politicians who serve them. The way the postmodern labour process shapes social, political, aesthetic and moral life has placed huge difficulties in the way of people taking control of their lives en masse. It is *these* problems which I shall focus on in future, but I believe that the way Marx used Hegel in *Capital* is a paradigm for understanding the most complex problems of human life.

The problems which humanity now faces still cannot be resolved without the removal of the "general stumbling block" (Marx 1844). This hasn't changed, and nor do I think there is any serious revision of *Capital* which can help. It remains the case that capitalists pay their employees only enough to live on, irrespective of the value of their product, pocket the unpaid labour and share it with their "hostile brothers" (Marx 1867).

The impending collapse of the natural systems which support human life can readily be shown to overshadow any other question faced by humanity. But neither capitalist exploitation nor environmental destruction by industry can be solved until we can overcome the problem of collective self-determination of human communities, presently bewildered and disorganised by the productive forces unleashed by capitalism. The real problems we face now go beyond the economic structure.

But we can learn from Marx and Hegel.

CHAPTER 1

Marx's Sources

1 Hegel's Theory of Science

Marxists have long recognised that Marx made use of Hegel's *Science of Logic* in his political economic studies and the writing of *Capital*. However, none have been able to explain *how* Marx used the *Logic* in *Capital*, as I demonstrated in my volume, *The Capital/Logic Debate* (2025).

The chief error of all these attempts generally was in presuming that Marx used the *Logic* as a metaphor or a model for political economy. As a result they looked for a homology or "likeness" between parts of *Capital* and parts of the *Logic*. But logic is a science which is distinguished from all other sciences by having no positive content. That is why Hegel began the *Logic* from an empty concept, Being, ensuring that no content would be smuggled into the Logic either by way of axioms or unacknowledged content implicit in the starting point.

Political Economy, however, like all the natural and human sciences, *has* a positive content. Both Hegel and Marx were well aware of this obvious fact. As Marx saw it, the content of Political Economy is value, that is, abstract human labour. Human labour, whether abstract or concrete, is not nothing. The whole of *Capital* depends on how Marx formulated the concept of abstract human labour.

If similarities in form between Hegel's *Logic* and any positive science can be found, this is because the sciences are made up of true concepts and all true concepts contain implicit contradictions characteristic of their subject matter. The way these contradictions originate and how they play out is bound to exhibit a variety of recognisable forms. Although every immanent exposition of a science, that is to say, an exposition which follows the logic of its content, is unique, similarities between sciences will always be found here and there. This is much like how each of the classic works of European music is unique and yet all share a multitude of those forms which are the subject matter of musicology. But recognising similarities is a far cry from understanding the logic which is unique to one phenomenon and one science.

Christopher Arthur is surely right when he said:

> So we have in the dialectic of capital one that is less general than Hegel's in its *scope*, but within its own terms equally *absolute* in so far as it is

> founded on all-round abstraction to leave quasilogical forms. Hegel's philosophy is encyclopaedic, and it has hundreds of categories accordingly. Capital, compared with the universe as a whole, is characterised by a poverty-stricken ontology.
>
> ARTHUR 2011

Hegel elaborated in the *Science of Logic* a range of more than 400 concepts and transitions from one concept to another from which the sciences he outlined in the *Encyclopaedia* could draw.

It is in the chapter of the *Logic*, entitled "The Idea of Cognition" that Hegel set out his theory for the development of the natural and human sciences. This chapter is the last before the chapter entitled "The Absolute Idea" which is merely a summary of the foregoing content. Any doubts about this claim can be laid to rest by examining the various sciences treated in outline in the *Encyclopaedia of the Philosophical Sciences*, all of which reflect the approach outlined in this passage both as a whole and in each individual science.

Christopher Arthur is the only participant in the *Capital / Logic* debate who noticed the existence of this chapter. Arthur wrote:

> What is striking is that this is thematised by Hegel in the part *preceding* the Absolute Idea, namely *cognition*. Here there *is* a discussion of how, in theory and in practice, the Idea both discovers, and creates, itself in what seems other than it. Yet by thematising this *before* the logical Absolute, Hegel makes it appear that success is guaranteed in advance.
>
> So I think that cognition should come at the end of the Logic, encapsulating the ambition of the concept to make itself Idea through uniting thought and reality, but with the job itself still to be done in the following parts of the *Encyclopaedia*. Cognition is surely the *hinge* of the logical and the real.
>
> ARTHUR, 2011

What Arthur overlooked in reading this passage is that the actor is not the Idea as such, but the "Subjective Notion," that is, a finite mind, which could be an individual person or a social movement or project such as Science, whose scientific activity is to be grasped insofar as it is necessary, and not psychologically. This finite mind has an urge (*Trieb*) or will to realise itself in the objective world, whose existence Hegel claims to prove in the Subjective Spirit. This drive to realise itself is the only element of the Philosophy of Spirit which is introduced into the *Logic*; there can be no sequence of concepts unless and until there is a subject which drives a concept beyond its limits in seeking to realise itself.

In §474 of the *Subjective Spirit*, Hegel concludes:

> What are the good and rational propensities, and how they are to be coordinated with each other? resolves itself into an exposition of the laws and forms of common life produced by the mind when developing itself as *objective mind* – a development in which the content of autonomous action loses its contingency and optionality. The discussion of the true intrinsic worth of the impulses, inclinations, and passions is thus essentially the theory of legal, moral, and social duties.
>
> HEGEL, 1831, §474

Consequently, human beings are driven to form a conceptual grasp of the Idea in the context of activity in a material world where it must have to do with "externality" as well as Logic. One path of this realisation of the will is outlined in the *Philosophy of Right*, Hegel's theory of modern society.

This is a problem which confronts all human beings, and it is one which can only be solved through the formation of a material culture by means of which human beings control their own will and some form of state which regulates the activity of themselves and other humans.

The outcome of the Idea of Cognition is the "Syllogism of Action," in which the subject uses one part of the objective world to act upon another to achieve its end. Thus the ambition of the Idea of Cognition is far more modest than the Absolute Idea, being simply to understand how human beings can rationally form concrete concepts of the world in which they live.

The passage entitled The Idea of Cognition sets out the means by which the *Encyclopaedia* and the various sciences outlined in the *Encyclopaedia* are to be constructed. A reading of the *Encyclopaedia* will confirm what Hegel says especially in the part of the Idea of Cognition called The Idea of the True.

Technology and the natural sciences were at such a primitive stage of development in Hegel's times that the application of Hegel's approach to the natural sciences raises problems which are irrelevant to the issues are raised by Marx's *Capital* and will not be considered here.

In Hegel's day there was no scientific theory for the development of the biosphere. Given that Hegel rejected the theory of Lamarck as implausible, the only available theory of the development of the world was that given in the Book of Genesis. Consequently, researchers of the time sought an anthropocentric rationality in the natural world. The evolution of the continents did become known in Hegel's life time, but that was the only clue Hegel had to the evolution of the Earth and the Universe as a whole. Further, microscopes were not yet powerful enough to reveal the microscopic world of life-forms which made explicable the life of the plants and animals encountered in human experience. In any case, Hegel did no original research in any of the natural sciences, he merely outlined their current forms in the Philosophy of Nature. His knowledge of the nervous system was also limited in the extreme and Psychology did not exist as a science in his time. Even in the social sciences, his knowledge of non-European societies was reliant on the reports of European missionaries and explorers and consequently was scant and Eurocentric.

Consequently, the only sciences which were genuinely open to Hegel were Logic and the Social Sciences, and in both these domains Hegel did epoch-making and original research. Hegel's *Philosophy of Right* is the only work of Hegel's on a positive science which stands up to criticism in our times, and provided Hegel with a field of research where all the essential facts were known to him. So this work provides the most fruitful exemplar of the theory of science outlined in the Idea of Cognition in the *Science of Logic*, and was the first work to which Marx turned when he "eagerly grasped the opportunity to withdraw from the public stage to my study" (1859).

I have provided an Appendix on my home page with annotated excerpts from "The Idea of the True." Below I will explain the passage in my own words.

1.1 *The Idea of the True*

In determining their action, a subject needs to know what is true of the object and which possible action promotes the Good. Accordingly, The Idea of Cognition is structured as a "syllogism," the two premises of which are The Idea of the True and the Idea of the Good. The action chosen by the subject will be in accord with both true and good.

The Idea of the True is itself a syllogism of which the first premise is Analytical Cognition and the second premise is Synthetic Cognition. That is, a science must represent a true concrete concept of the Object by an analysis of the object into parts and a synthesis of those parts according to a concept of the phenomenon.

The subject matter presents itself as a range of distinct phenomena which will each be known by some abstract general conception, such as "Right" or "Art" or "Political Economy," but none are yet grasped as a true concept. The conception which marks out each given phenomenon is characterised as "abstract general" because in the absence of a true, concrete concept, its conception will be based on such things as its place in human practice such as its usefulness, some common feature or quality of things given in perception or opinion, or its connection with other phenomena, or alternatively some problem or lack in respect to such features.

Analysis requires that any existing theory of the subject matter must be laid aside with the aim of forming a true concept of the phenomenon. The subject matter must be apprehended without any mediation, but taken up just as it immediately appears to "ordinary consciousness."

Ordinary consciousness has at its disposal universal and particular conceptions (which can be used provisionally) and concrete individual moments which are given immediately in perception, one of which is distinctive in some way and needs explaining. This is the starting point of a science.

Initially, the subject must make itself passive before the subject matter (object) so that the subject matter is able to *show itself* without the imposition of any preconceptions on the part of the subject. Analysis continues as far as is possible to find the smallest elements which can be taken as part of the subject matter, arranging them according to differences and commonalities found in the subject matter, but without any overall plan or concept of the material.

Initially, it doesn't matter how the material is organised, just so long as its concreteness is retained, because the organisation of material can always be revised later. Analysis is complete when the smallest element is isolated which counts as part of the subject matter as conceived in the abstract general understanding of the phenomenon and the complete diversity of these elements is elaborated. Analysis does not go beyond the point where the whole which makes an elementary part of the phenomenon is surpassed. For example, analysis of social phenomena would not go beyond the individual human being to parts of the body, because all social phenomena are taken as essentially relations between whole human beings and their activity.

In Hegel's words:

> Analytic cognition ... starts from a *presupposed*, and therefore individual, *concrete* subject matter; this may be an object already *complete in itself* for ordinary thought, or it may be a *problem*, that is to say, given only in its circumstances and conditions, but not yet disengaged from them and presented on its own account in simple self-subsistence. (§1709)

"Complete in itself" means that the object is not seen as a part or result of some larger phenomenon but is immediately given to everyday consciousness. The criteria by which the material can be arranged is arbitrary but must be immanent to the subject matter itself. Criteria from outside the individual datum must not be introduced because this would prematurely entail some form of mediation. Only what is immediate is to be retained.

Analysis continues until the full range of data belonging to the phenomenon is identified and arranged according to its immanent differences. The principle of analysis, its outcome and the guiding principle of analysis, is the One. The One is a "relationless atom." Analysis is nothing other than an apprehension of what *is*.

Generally speaking the concepts elaborated in the Logic of Being in the *Science of Logic* are applicable to analysis. This is not to say that analysis will *replicate* the Logic of Being, but simply that analysis draws on these concepts. However, the conceptions are now not merely formal, as they are in the Logic of Being, but have *content*. That content comes from the concrete individual products of analysis. Analysis establishes what *is* and that is not Nothing, as it is in the *Logic*.

When analysis is complete, cognition passes over to synthesis in which products of analysis are brought into relation with one another. There is inevitably a movement back and forth between analysis and synthesis because each analysis is provisional.

> Synthetic cognition aims at the *comprehension* of what *is*, that is, at grasping the multiplicity of determinations in their unity, ultimately as determinations of the same concept. It is therefore the second premise of the syllogism in which the *diverse* as such is related. Hence its aim is in general *necessity* ... Now synthetic cognition passes over, in the first instance, *from abstract identity to relation*. (§1720)

During this phase of cognition the concepts elaborated in the Essence Logic will be utilised, as demonstrated when Hegel talks of the movement from abstract Identity to relation. But again, it must be emphasised not by means of some kind of replica of this section of the *Logic*. The concepts which will be used in the first phase of synthesis will resemble those found in this section of the *Logic* which begins with a *critique of Identity*. But this development is still not guided by a concrete concept of the subject matter, even though it is understood that the determinations given are those of the Notion. With the Subjective Notion, the concept is still in development. The development of this phase may take the form of an immanent critique of existing theories which have hitherto been held in abeyance. The *outcome* of this phase is to be a true concept of the phenomenon, marking the beginning of a new division of science. In a sense, up to this point we are still in the "pre-scientific" phase of analysis of a phenomenon.

The key paragraph comes under the heading of "Division." In this context, Political Economy figures as one division, but the same principles also apply to divisions *within* Political Economy.

The problem is how to choose *which* individual product of analysis is to be the starting point for the synthesis of a new "circle," that is to say, a new science which will take the form of a concrete concept of the phenomenon analysed.

Recall that all such products of analysis will be as given above in §1709: "a *presupposed*, and therefore individual, *concrete* subject matter ... an object already *complete in itself* for ordinary thought."

> The progress, proper to the Notion, from universal to particular, is the basis and the possibility of a *synthetic science*, of a *system* and of *systematic cognition*. (§1733)

But when starting from the universal, Hegel is still referring to some concrete product of analysis – the single instance which expresses universal. Consequently, the subject must select from among the products of analysis a "universal individual" as follows:

> The first requisite for this is, as we have shown, that the beginning be made with the subject matter in the form of a *universal*. In the sphere of actuality, whether of nature or spirit, it is the concrete individuality that is given to subjective, natural cognition as the *prius* (*das Erste*, i.e., first); but in cognition that is a *comprehension* (*Begreifen*), at least to the extent that it has the form of the Notion (*Begriff*) for basis, the *prius* must be on the contrary something *simple* (*Einfach*), something *abstracted* (*Ausgeschiedene*) from the concrete, because in this form alone has the subject-matter the form of the self-related universal or of an immediate based on the Notion. (§1734)

Note in the above that this requirement is limited to "the sphere of actuality, whether of nature or spirit." In other words, natural science and the human sciences, anything but Logic. However, the equivalent concept in the *Logic* is the One – a contentless unit.

The universal individual (the prius or first) is selected from amongst other individual data on the basis that it expresses in its own nature what is universal in the phenomenon. This depends on how the subject conceives of the phenomenon, but this is not a matter of personal opinion but reflects existing science or social movement. Marx's choice of the commodity was in this sense equally a product of an immanent critique of political economy as an analysis of the subject matter itself, in particular his study of economic history.

Since the universal individual must be a "concrete individuality" alongside other particular individuals, "value" does not qualify. "Value" is already a product of synthesis which draws together and generalises diverse parts of the subject matter of political economy, which are in turned taken to be "forms of value." "Value" is not given to immediate perception. The choice of the universal individual is limited to individual concrete objects of "subjective, natural cognition."

This datum is called the first or original, in German *das Erste*, but translated by Miller as the "prius," a word which is not commonly known, so I prefer to retain the term "first" for this unit, the "One" of political economy.

Hegel says that the first must be "something *simple*, something *abstracted* (*Ausgeschiedene*) from the concrete." Analysis has already produced the simplest possible data which qualify as components of the given phenomenon, in this case, the simplest elements of political economic activity. Hegel says that the unit must be abstracted from the concrete, so the historically simplest, most primitive instance of the entity must be chosen and abstracted from the concrete and taken up in its own essential nature. That is, what is identical in any stage of development of the economic environment, even though it is universal for only one economic system. For this reason, Marx set aside commodities in the particular forms of a service or an ideal (such as intellectual property), taking as its universal, or archetype, the simple material product of human labour characteristic of industrial capitalism. The commodity in this universal form was known before Political Economy, from the earliest times of human society, albeit as a marginal and extraneous part of ancient life. It is self-related in that it does not depend on any other product of analysis for its being, it stands on its own, complete in itself, so to speak.

It was on this basis that Marx selected the commodity. This universal individual can be termed the *unit* (*Einzelheit*) as well as the *germ cell* (*der Keim*), both terms which Hegel uses in the *Logic*. Unit, because it is the One, the simplest and final complete product of analysis of the subject matter of political economy; germ cell because analysis of the commodity will be the conceptual basis guiding the resynthesis of political economy as a consistent, concrete science, and is in this sense the embryonic form of a series of forms of value which grow out of it.

> the form of abstract universality is characteristic of its *first*. Therefore any subject matter whatever that seems to possess an elementary universality is made the subject matter of a specific science, and is an absolute beginning to the extent that *ordinary thought is presupposed* to be acquainted with it and it is taken on its own account as requiring no derivation. (§1738)

What remains then is the analysis of the final product of analysis of political economy. Analysis of this datum, the commodity, is a unique scientific task, producing a new *universal* concept.

As to the synthesis of the products of analysis, Hegel says that there are no given criteria for how *particulars* are to be defined.

> Only an immanent principle would be required, that is, a beginning from the universal and the Notion ... and therefore takes the determinateness of the content from what is given. ... For the particular that makes its appearance in division, there is no ground of its own available, either in regard to what is to constitute the basis of the division. (§1739)

> ... there exists a crowd of principles to which it has to conform, and therefore in one series of its forms follows one principle, and in other series other principles, as well as producing hybrids. (§1740)

Each division of the subject matter, moving from the universal individual or unit, to each *particular* unit, must be made in the same way as described. This means that not only must the commodity be analysed and provide the basis for further development, but at *each stage* in the synthesis a new first (or unit or gem cell) must be chosen which will function as a unit and germ cell for further development.

In composing the *Encyclopaedia*, Hegel identified the unit of each science in the form of a limit, contradiction, product or aporia in the preceding science, as illustrated in the case of the *Philosophy of Right* whose germ cell is a fundamental unit of Objective Spirit, a unit of private property (according to Hegel). This unit is a product of Hegel's *Philosophy of Subjective Spirit*.

However, Marx can make no such assumptions about "human nature," with or without a natural philosophy to justify it. The *Encyclopaedia* is not available to the modern writer who therefore cannot count, as Hegel did, on the validity of an underlying science. In lieu of this, the present day scientist must have recourse to the historical development of the object itself and in its reflection in the science of the time. "The real subject retains its autonomous existence outside the head just as before" (Marx, 1857, p. 101).

According to Hegel, analysis of the germ cell provides a concrete universal concept of the subject matter *in nuce*, and further progress towards the determination of particulars is to be guided by the products of the analysis of the germ cell, which obliges us to turn to Marx's use of history.

1.2 *Hegel's Social Theory*

The first work to which Marx turned when he "eagerly grasped the opportunity to withdraw from the public stage to my study" (1859) was *The Philosophy of Right* (Hegel, 1821). In this work, Hegel developed what is widely recognised as a social theory in the form of a discourse on *ethics*. How we live is answered by Hegel in the frame of how we *should* live rather than how we are forced to live by economic or social "forces." It is a work of moral philosophy rather than what is normally expected of social science in our times. This was not eccentric in Hegel's times, however. Rousseau's theory is also more a moral theory than a "social science," and Adam Smith made his name for *Theory of the Moral Sentiments* before he wrote *The Wealth of Nations*.

The main syllogism which makes up the structure of *The Philosophy of Right* is composed of three successive ethical realms.

1.3 *Right*

The first stage of the *Philosophy of Right* is Right, which Hegel characterises by the aphorism: "Hence the imperative of right is: 'Be a person and respect others as persons'" (§36). The subject arrives on the scene, so to speak, with a natural will, that is, a will of the kind we have in common with the animal kingdom, but with an intellect which is capable of transcending this indeterminate natural will. "The will therefore becomes a single will, a person" (§34). This transition to being a person happens, in Hegel's view, through *private property*. The person knows themself as an object by making themselves objective in their property and being recognised as such by other persons, whose property rights are recognised in turn. Thus simple, immediate *possession* is transformed into a judicial relation by the recognition of a person's private property by all other persons. This is what Hegel meant by "respecting others as persons."

On the basis of the concept of property, Hegel builds up a framework of rights to own property including property in one's own body which is inalienable, and the entire apparatus of civil and criminal law.

Simply put, this first regime of "abstract right" is what has been characterised, most famously by Isaiah Berlin, as "negative rights" – sometimes called "liberty" – you can do anything you like so long as you don't violate the rights of others.

1.4 *Morality*

The second stage of conceptual reconstruction of the modern state in Hegel's theory is Morality. Here the person becomes a *moral subject*. Note the confusing new usage of the word "subject." The formerly indeterminate will of a *natural* subject is transcended by the person which is now in turn transcended by the *moral* subject.

The moral subject is distinguished from the right-bearing person because they consult their own conscience when deciding upon an action. The moral subject is responsible for the foreseeable impact of their action on others irrespective of what is dictated by property rights. Hegel uses the problem of lighting a fire on your own property to illustrate how unexpected consequences for others can result from a private action.

In general, Freedom cannot be achieved in a world in which everyone simply respects each other's rights, but is dependent on raising the moral and cultural level of the entire community. The moral subject realises that their own welfare can only be pursued by having a mind to the welfare of others. The problem of unforeseen consequences of one's actions however highlights the fact that the moral subject cannot know what will ultimately prove to serve the general good. The subject guided solely by their own conscience may equally well do evil as do good in the world. Even while abstract right is respected, there is no criterion within Morality which can distinguish between good and evil.

This contradiction leads to the highest ethical plane, the citizen and their state.

1.5 *The State and Ethical Life*

Hegel says "ethical life (*Sittlichkeit*) is the concept of freedom developed into the existing world" (§142). This means that the State, which is the actual embodiment of many generations of ethical experience: "posits within itself distinctions whose specific character is thereby determined by the concept, and which endow the ethical order with a stable content independently necessary and subsistent in exaltation above subjective opinion and caprice. These distinctions are absolutely valid laws and institutions" (§144).

Hegel did not agree with Marx and Lenin or, to be honest, most ordinary people today, that the state is an instrument for the defence of certain material interests. On the contrary, the state was for Hegel the real embodiment of the will of the people. This notwithstanding that Hegel did not believe in universal suffrage; he believed that universal suffrage was a delusion, decisions would always be made by small cabals and the single vote made in private never amounted to anything.

In Hegel's view, that State is the pinnacle of an entire "collegial" structure in which the people expressed their will through voluntary associations based on their trade and so forth. Unlike the moral subject, the citizen was not an abstract individual but on the contrary was a member of a definite estate and/or corporation and family; the citizen contributed to the state according to the particular social position they had in society.

These three moral realms coexist in Hegel's view of the modern state. Every subject has the right to own property and has bodily autonomy; as a moral subject each has the duty to decide on their own action through moral reflection; every citizen is obliged to participate in the state and its institutions according to their social position and the law. This is how a Hegelian syllogism works – all three propositions are simultaneously true and obligatory, even though each has a different basis and may be in conflict with each other.

Marx was famously dismissive of ethics and moral philosophy, which is a shame, because this hostility to ethics became common parlance in the Communist Parties of the twentieth century and provided cover for all sorts of outrageous behaviour. Nevertheless, by the 1960s this mistake started to be recognised, and I think George Brenkert (1983) was right when he claimed that Marx advocated for an ethic of freedom and that *Capital* ought to be read as a work of moral philosophy as much as a work of political economy.

2 Marx's Use of History

One sense in which Hegel was an Idealist is that Hegel overestimated the power of the reasoning of an individual person. Hegel was the last great encyclopaedic thinker. But most of his *Encyclopaedia of the Philosophical Sciences* was simply a rationalisation of existing sciences, and did not represent original research on his own behalf. After Hegel, no one else tried to emulate his *Encyclopaedia*. Each science was pursued relatively independently of the others, and connections between the sciences were allowed to emerge of themselves with the passage of time.

The *Encyclopaedia* was described by Hegel as a "circle of circles." Each science (or form of life) was complete and consistent within itself but nonetheless always generated some "undecidable" question, some question which arose within the science which could not be answered within its own terms. Twentieth century mathematicians recovered this idea in the context of mathematical theories with Kurt Gödel's Incompleteness Theorem. It was by this means that each circle in the *Encyclopaedia* generated the concept which provided the starting point for the next circle.

However, no one after Hegel had the benefit of such an encyclopaedia. Identifying the unit which was to be the embryo of a new science cannot simply rely on being able to read it off an aporia in the "preceding" or underlying science. While an individual thinker cannot devise a complete encyclopaedia, this limitation does not apply to the "real subject." "The real historical process" (Marx, 1857, p. 101, 102) suffers no such limitation. However, a particular kind of historical investigation is required to determine concepts as they are realised and constructed within the historical process.

Analysis of the concepts of Political Economy must be informed by a study of the real historical process by means of which each of these "simplest economic categories" came about. It is in fact impossible to perceive and understand any complex social entity without understanding the history which produced it. To believe that you can conceptually reconstruct a given social formation simply by the application of logic to actuality is an Hegelian illusion which Marx did not share.

Capital is not an historical work (though it does have a couple of historical chapters), but a deep study of economic history was necessary in order to well understand the concepts of political economy, and in particular to determine the *prius*, the starting point of the sequence of concepts to be elaborated, and the nodal concepts which follow. Of course, if you believe that *Capital* is a work of Logic, then there would be no place in it for the study of history. On the contrary though, if the concepts of political economy, unlike the concepts of Logic, have a *content*, then it is impossible to grasp them without knowing the history through which they acquired that content. Who could understand the Treaty of Versailles if they didn't know that it was drafted by the victorious powers in World War One?

Christopher Arthur says:

> I draw a distinction between systematic dialectic (which is a method of exhibiting the inner articulation of a given whole) and historical dialectic (which is a method of exhibiting the inner connection between stages of development of a temporal process).
>
> ARTHUR, 2011

and

> The effort is to deploy a systematic dialectic in order to articulate the relations of a given social order, namely capitalism, as opposed to a historical dialectic studying the rise and fall of social systems.
>
> ARTHUR, 2011

But it is wrong to assert a dichotomy or opposition between a systematic dialectic on one hand and the dialectic of the rise and fall of economic relations on the historical plane on the other – doubly so if attention is confined to whichever economic relation is dominant in successive epochs. The historical dialectic which is of interest is the development of each single economic relation taken on its own.

Insofar as the demise of a social system is intelligible, and not due simply to some external or accidental cause, then the key to understanding that demise lies precisely in the tendencies revealed by systematic dialectic. However, the point is that, while an economic system is generally consistent within itself and able to cope with internal conflicts within the economic system as such, this is not true of the relations of the economic to *other* circles of human practice. The economic whole is but a *part* of the totality of human practice, of human social life in Nature.

It is in the nature of a systematic whole that it is able to reproduce itself out of its conditions despite changes in those conditions. However, this capacity is finite. At some point, other aspects of a form of life go beyond the limit of what is capable of supporting a given economic regime. This is analogous to an organism which continues to reproduce itself despite disruptions in its environment, but only up to a point. Wherever we find secular tendencies in a system, that is, tendencies which are not equilibrated by other tendencies, then crisis will inevitably follow.

In the absence of his own *Encyclopaedia*, and in the spirit of a philosophy of which the substance is human activity (or practices), Marx relied on the work of the "real subject" which "retains its autonomous existence outside the head":

> In the succession of the economic categories, as in any other historical, social science, it must not be forgotten that their subject – here, modern bourgeois society – is always what is given, in the head as well as in reality, and that these categories therefore express the forms of being, the characteristics of existence, and often only individual sides of this specific society, this subject, and that therefore this society by no means

> begins only at the point where one can speak of it *as such*; this holds *for science as well*. This is to be kept in mind because it will shortly be decisive for the order and sequence of the categories.
>
> MARX, 1857, p. 106

Yes, the sequence of categories is different in the systematic elaboration of an economic system from their sequence as dominant relations in the real history of economic systems. But that is not the question at issue. The determination of the logic of political economy requires a study of the historical development of each of those relations themselves, abstracted from their economic conditions, and not just their periods of dominance.

This is different from the kind of history done by professional historians who prefer to study forms of life as a whole and eschew narratives spanning across large stretches of time. The kind of history needed is more akin to genealogy in that it traces the line of development of a particular relationship as the world changes around it, and it does so from the point of interest in the present, rather than in its own terms in any given epoch, as would normally be required by the professional historian.

It is also true, as Arthur says, that the capitalist economy is conceived by Marx as a systematic, self-reproducing whole, and that an exposition of this system cannot include an examination of production within its scope. Technique proceeds apace according to its own laws, although always with the stimulus or constraint of the political and economic system in which technical and scientific activity takes place.

The economic system determines the various economic forms in which the products of the system of production will be represented in the economy but does not as such determine production, which is a unique form of interaction between humans and Nature, the subject matter of the science of technique. Within the Earth's natural system as a whole, the only genuinely self-reproducing, self-adapting systematic whole is the entirety of human practice. Not its economic or political systems alone. Within the system of human practice, economic activity, technique, science, reproductive activity, art, etc., are each a *relatively* self-reproducing system, all of which interact with one another. The system of technique on which an economic system rests may be more or less independent, more or less insulated against external disturbances. But at some point the capacity of the economic activity will be exhausted.

> At a certain stage of development, the material productive forces of society come into conflict with the existing relations of production or – this

> merely expresses the same thing in legal terms – with the property relations within the framework of which they have operated hitherto. From forms of development of the productive forces these relations turn into their fetters. Then begins an era of social revolution. The changes in the economic foundation lead sooner or later to the transformation of the whole immense superstructure.
>
> Preface, MARX, 1859

It is not necessary to go so far as "social revolution." The development of technique is continuously disrupting the social relations within which production is taking place. In itself, bourgeois economy is a self-sustaining system, but it cannot ensure for itself a stable technical relation to Nature, and consequently, nor a stable social and political environment. On the contrary, unlike all previous economic systems, capitalism continuously stimulates the revolutionising of the techniques of production, and the political conditions which make capital accumulation possible are subject to unceasing change in the economic system. Capitalism continuously exacerbates inequality and concentrates wealth in the hands of a few, threatening the social and political presuppositions for its own existence.

Hegel conceived of the *whole* – in my reading, the entirety of human practice – as a "circle of circles." Hegel was unaware that the natural environment in which human beings lived was itself a product of evolution. Consequently, the entirety of human practice he saw as an absolutely self-reproducing system, but no subordinate part of that whole was absolutely self-reproducing.

Marx wanted to discover how the relations between the economic system. the political system and production system would be disrupted. For this a preparatory study of history was required.

2.1 *Categorical Genealogy*

I will coin the term *categorical genealogy* for the type of historical investigation which was necessary before Marx could determine the logical relations between the various concepts of the political economy of bourgeois society. I carried out an investigation of this kind with the object not of economic life, but of political life. This was published as *The Origins of Collective Decision Making* (2015). Although I set off from problems which were being manifested in present-day political life, the genealogical investigation of the categories of collective decision making shed entirely new light on present-day political life.

In approaching a critique of the existing science of Political Economy Marx needed to investigate the history of each of its categories, a project which is quite distinct from critique of the various systems of Political Economy.

This is also self-evidently a task entirely different from investigating the history of dominant economic formations, the usual subject matter of economic history and what Arthur was referring to above as "the historical dialectic."

In particular, Marx needed to investigate the history of the concept of "value" and its various social forms, in particular but not limited to, the commodity, money, capital, the working day and rent.

The results of his genealogical study of value-forms up to and including the commodity are briefly presented in §3 of Chapter 1 of *Capital*, where it is already presented in logical form and demonstrably shaped by the concrete understanding of value which Marx had arrived at by the time of writing *Capital*. His "categorical genealogy" is a merging of both logical and historical investigation.

It is well-documented that commodity exchange was marginal in ancient times; travellers and itinerant merchants and neighbouring peoples provided only occasional exotic products. In early mediaeval times, market activity was tightly regulated by the monarchy and restricted to monthly markets and later restricted to the growing towns. In late mediaeval times, the flow of products from other countries gradually undermined traditional guild control of production. In these times, there was no clear distinction between a working class and a bourgeoisie; these were merely the better-off or poorer sections of the merchant and artisan classes gradually developing in the towns, trading in agricultural produce purchased from the peasantry and the products of artisans.

Gradually, differentiation between masters or proprietors and wealthy merchants on one hand, and labourers, journeymen and apprentices on the other, began to widen, especially with the growth of colonialism. Merchant companies like the East India Company became enormously wealthy whilst the monarchy, saddled with expensive business of waging war and maintaining order became relatively impoverished and had to borrow from the now burgeoning bourgeoisie.

The creation of an impoverished proletariat in the cities as a result of the Enclosures and the existence of significant accumulations of capital as a result of colonial trade provided the conditions for industrial capitalism to take root. These were the conditions which led to the revolutions of the seventeenth and eighteenth centuries which ultimately put the bourgeoisie in political power and would make the commodity-form the dominant economic relation in modern society. Early concentrations of workers in large workshops gradually gave way to full-blown industrial capitalist exploitation.

The above narrative is not of course a good exemplar of the work of the historian. But "it is not necessary to write the *real history of the relations of production*" (Marx, 1857, p. 460).

> Once production founded on capital is presupposed ... its *historic presuppositions*, which, precisely as such *historic* presuppositions, are past and gone, and hence belong to the *history of its formation*, but in no way to its *contemporary* history, i.e. not to the real system of the mode of production ruled by it. ... While e.g. the flight of serfs to the cities is one of the *historic* conditions and presuppositions of urbanism, it is not a *condition*, they therefore disappear as real capital arises, capital which itself, on the basis of its own reality, posits the conditions for its realization. ... These presuppositions, which originally appeared as conditions of its becoming – and hence could not spring from its *action as capital* – now appear as results of its own realization, reality, as *posited by it – not as conditions of its arising, but as results of its presence*. ... These indications, together with a correct grasp of the present, then also offer the key to the understanding of the past ... In order to develop the laws of bourgeois economy, therefore, it is not necessary to write the *real history of the relations of production*. But the correct observation and deduction of these laws, as having themselves become in history, always leads to primary equations ... which point towards a past lying behind this system.
>
> MARX, 1857, pp. 459–460

Thus Marx was able to determine that the commodity was not only the simplest form of value, but it appeared long before and independently of the bourgeois and was the chief process which paved the way for the growth of the bourgeoisie and the dominance of capital. Further, capital did not just exploit the existence of an impoverished mass of proletarians, but actively and continuously reproduced and expanded the working class, earning just enough each day to be able to return to work the next day. Capital now did not merely organise industrial workers under one roof, but actively drove the continuous revolutionisation of the techniques of production.

In short, Marx had to study the history of the commodity, of capital, wages and so on, the various forms of value, in order to understand their essential nature and their relation to one another – their genealogy in other words.

3 Marx's Critique of Ricardo

Marx began his study of Political Economy as early as 1843 with his "Comments on James Mill," and continued through to the publication of the first volume of *Capital* in 1867, with several extended breaks when illness and the demands of agitational and political work overtook his economic studies. (Marx rarely allowed the exigencies of earning a living interrupt his work).

In line with the method of immanent critique which he learnt from Hegel (the Introduction to the *Encyclopaedia Logic* is the best example of Hegel's use of this method), Marx examined each work in detail, tracing the reasoning of each writer and each dispute and followed the course of the science, diagnosed its failure to produce a genuine science, and sought a way forward.

Marx credited William Petty (1623–1687) with having been the first to have attempted to build a *system* of concepts with his *Political Arithmetik*. The giants of the field were Adam Smith whose *Wealth of Nations was* published in 1776 and David Ricardo whose *On The Principles of Political Economy and Taxation* was published in 1817.

> Political economy had achieved a certain comprehensiveness with Adam Smith; to a certain extent he had covered the whole of its territory, so that Say was able to summarise it all in one textbook, superficially but quite systematically.
>
> MARX, 1863, chapter 10

It was Adam Smith who first formulated the labour theory of value. According to Ricardo:

> It has been observed by Adam Smith, that 'the word Value has two different meanings, and sometimes expresses the utility of some particular object, and sometimes the power of purchasing other goods which the possession of that object conveys. The one may be called value in use; the other value in exchange.'
>
> RICARDO, 1817, citing SMITH, 1776, Book 1, Chapter 4

What Smith perceived as ambiguity is in fact the marker of a true concept. It is not the case that value has two *alternative* meanings, but rather that the concept of value is the necessary coincidence of two processes, and it is this connection alone which can form the basis for a true concept of value, not one or the other independently.

> 'The real price of every thing,' says Adam Smith, 'what every thing really costs to the man who wants to acquire it, is the toil and trouble of acquiring it. What every thing is really worth to it, or the man who has acquired it, and who wants to dispose of it, or exchange it for something else, is the toil and trouble which it can save to himself, and which it can impose upon other people.' 'Labour was the first price – the original purchase-money that was paid for all things.'
>
> op. cit, citing SMITH, 1776, Book 1, Chapter 5

Smith however made no attempt to make this observation into the founding principle of Political Economy. He mixed it up with sundry empirical observations, and like almost all Political Economists to follow, held that rather than having a single substance, value had multiple sources apart from labour – the land, the capital itself borrowed to establish the enterprise, and the "inspection and direction" (1776, Book 1, Ch 6) of the capitalist. Each source had to be rewarded respectively with rent, interest, profit and wages with these diverse components each contributing to value.

Ricardo, on the other hand, declared in the subheading of Chapter 1, "On Value" of his *Principles*:

> The value of a commodity, or the quantity of any other commodity for which it will exchange, depends on the relative quantity of labour which is necessary for its production, and not on the greater or less compensation which is paid for that labour.
>
> RICARDO, 1817, Chapter 1

He then endeavoured to show that "each separate form of wealth must be understood as modifications of one and the same universal substance rather than simply described." (Marx, *Theories of Surplus Value*, 1863, Ch. 10)

But rather than building his theory step by step from his definition of value:

> In this first chapter not only are *commodities* assumed to exist – and when considering value as such, nothing further is required – but also wages, capital, profit, the general rate of profit and even … the various forms of capital as they arise from the process of circulation, and also the difference between 'natural and market-price'.
>
> MARX, Theories of Surplus Value, 1863, Ch. 10

In that same Chapter One, "the permanent rate of profits" was taken as a given datum. A more or less uniform rate of profit across the entire economy was an empirical fact. However, by introducing as simply something given at the very outset of his theory, without any derivation of its level from basic principles, Ricardo undermined the basis of the theory he wanted to build.

Ricardo showed that a general rise in wages will necessarily result *not* in a rise in the price of commodities, as is widely believed to this day, but rather a corresponding reduction in the rate of profit. However, Ricardo never derived the general rate of profit from his theory of value, but merely took it as a given datum as if it arose from the customs and habits of the people, just as "the natural price of labour … essentially depends on the habits and customs of the people" (1817, Ch. 5).

Likewise, the money-commodity was posited right away in Chapter 1 without any reflection on the origin of money, its nature or the multiple functions which money performs in a capitalist economy.

Marx was clear that identification of a single principle which made every species of value in bourgeois society a modification of one universal substance was the necessary basis for the formation of political economy as a science. Wages, money, capital, interest, profit all had to be *derived* as forms of value and their nature and relation to each other determined in this way.

Working through Ricardo's work line-by-line Marx identified frequent logical errors. His categories were not clearly formed and shifted their meaning from one chapter to another; he distinguished, as was the custom, between fixed and circulating capital – categories which fail to distinguish between what Marx called constant capital (which Ricardo wrongly equated with "fixed capital") and variable capital; value was confused with cost price; he always considered the length of the working day as a fixed quantity; he frequently used examples in which constant capital was assumed to be zero, obscuring the different between the rate of surplus value and the rate of profit. This failure to account for the difference between the quantity of profit as a proportion of total capital invested, and the same absolute quantity as a proportion of living labour employed Marx saw as a crucial failure.

These weakness were evident not to Marx alone, but were the basis which Ricardo's opponents used to dismiss his theory. On the other hand, Ricardo's followers tried to "fix" the theory by ridding it of its contradictions, but in so doing, Marx observed, they undermined the very basis of Ricardo's theory. As a result, Political Economy went into decline, eventually abandoning Ricardo's effort to bring political economy under a single unifying principle in the concept of value.

However, the fact remained that a labour theory of value was in direct contradiction to a uniform general rate of profit, both written into his theory from the very beginning, meaning that contradictions *could not* be eliminated from Ricardo's theory without destroying the theory as a whole. The reality of capitalism itself contains a contradiction and this contradiction had to be made explicit in the theory.

Further,

> *Ricardo does not examine* the form – the peculiar characteristic of labour that creates exchange-value or manifests itself in exchange-values – the *nature* of this labour. Hence he does not grasp the connection of *this labour* with *money* or that it must assume the form of *money*.
>
> MARX, 1863, ch 10

The chief task in front of Marx in composing *Capital* was to make the labour theory of value into the consistent, unifying, scientific principle of Political Economy, and *derive* the nature of money, capital and the general rate of profit as an outcome of the theory. Marx also needed to be able to advise the workers' movement as to how the living standards of workers could be advanced and identify tendencies toward crisis inherent in bourgeois society which would provide the conditions for the overthrow of capital.

The most challenging task Marx faced was how to retain the integrity of the labour theory of value and yet derive the uniform general rate of profit which stands in direct contradiction to the labour theory of value. To overcome this problem he had to turn to Hegel.

3.1 *The Three Sources and Component Parts of* Capital

I have briefly outlined the three sources of Marx's approach to composing *Capital*. I will show that the structure and logic of the whole work is shaped by Marx's appropriation of Hegel's *Logic*, especially the section analysed above, "The Idea of the True." It will be seen that Marx's division of *Capital* into Parts explicitly reflects his appropriation of this passage, which Hegel applied in shaping the structure of his *Encyclopaedia* and its divisions.

Further, like Hegel, Marx did not simply construct a system of his own and counterpose it to rival theories. On the contrary, he read through the entire literature of Political Economy and diagnosed its failure to build a consistent system of capitalist economics as it had aimed to do. He identified the specific problems which remained unsolved in the work of the best effort to create such a system, that of Ricardo. Solving these outstanding problems had to be addressed in *Capital*, and to do this he critically appropriated the concepts developed by the Political Economists. In this sense he positioned *Capital* as a continuation of Political Economy, but took it beyond its own limitations.

His crucial break from Hegel and the Political Economists was his study of the *history* of each of the forms of value, each to be understood in its own nature, even when it was peripheral in relation to the dominant economic formation.

In the immediately following chapters I will simply précis the three volumes of *Capital*. After this I will present a brief summary in which the structure of *Capital* is made explicit, and Marx's use of "The Idea of the True" is clear.

Also evident from this chapter is how Marx's claim that the contradiction between the rate of surplus value and the uniform rate of profit is a real contradiction which cannot therefore be eliminated but is reflected in *Capital*.

CHAPTER 2

Capital

1 Marx's *Capital* Volume One: the Process of Production of Capital

1.1 *Part 1. Commodities and Money*

1.1.1 Chapter 1 §1, the Two Factors of a Commodity: Use-Value and Value

> The wealth of those societies in which the capitalist mode of production prevails, presents itself as "an immense accumulation of commodities," its unit being a single commodity. Our investigation must therefore begin with the analysis of a commodity.
>
> MARX, 1867

With these words Marx began the first section of Chapter 1, subtitled "The Two Factors of a Commodity: Use-value and value (The substance of value and the magnitude of value)."

The Political Economists had shown that political economy is the science of value. Marx shows that the commodity, the simplest form of value, well known to the ordinary consciousness of any denizen of bourgeois society, is the *unit* and substance of wealth, and the *prius* or starting point for the building of a system of political economy as a whole. Provided all other forms of value can be shown to be particular species of commodity, then the commodity also represents the Universal. All just as Hegel advised.

Like Ricardo, who began with "Chapter 1. Value," and claimed that all the features of bourgeois society were forms of value, Marx began his system of political economy from value, but he specifically begins from the simplest social form of value found in bourgeois society, the commodity (Marx, 1881), and from *this alone*. There is no mention of money until §3 of Chapter 1, let alone price, wages, capital and so on. In contrast, Ricardo had introduced these other basic concepts from the very beginning, as empirically given facts. Marx will focus his attention on analysis of this basic and historically first form of value, and move on to deriving other, more developed forms of value only later in the work – moving from the universal to the particular and from the abstract to the concrete.

To proceed from this beginning, Marx analysed the commodity, and revealed its internal contradiction (just as Hegel did in the *Encyclopaedia*) in order to create the basis to synthesise all the other concepts of political economy.

> The utility of a thing makes it a use value. ... independent of the amount of labour required ... Use values become a reality only by use or consumption: they also constitute the substance of all wealth, whatever may be the social form of that wealth. ... they are, in addition, the material depositories of exchange value.
>
> loc. cit.

In fact, a commodity must be of use to *someone else* other than the producer in order to be a commodity and have exchange value. But while its use-value is indifferent to the quantity of labour required to produce it, its exchange-value does depend on the quantity of labour embodied in its production.

> Exchange value, at first sight, presents itself as a quantitative relation, as the proportion in which values in use of one sort are exchanged for those of another sort ... the exchange values of commodities must be capable of being expressed in terms of something common to them all, of which thing they represent a greater or less quantity. ... If then we leave out of consideration the use value of commodities, they have only one common property left, that of being products of labour. ... all are reduced to one and the same sort of labour, human labour in the abstract. ... When looked at as crystals of this social substance, common to them all, they are – Values.
>
> loc. cit.

In this first section, Marx shows that the value of a commodity is determined by the socially average labour-time required for its production by consideration of the division of the whole social labour. He makes no mention of price at this point.

Under conditions where labour is more productive and therefore can produce the same use-value in less time, then the value of each commodity is reduced correspondingly. It is not the *actual* labour expended on producing a given commodity which gives that commodity its value, but rather the *average* labour time, or, from the point of view of the economy as a whole, the total labour time required to produce all of the given products required. This value is determined through the process of exchange on the market and is realised (appears) only at the moment of exchange.

A commodity produced for one's own consumption is useful but does not have *value*; likewise, the tithe-corn provided by a peasant for the feudal landlord does not have value because it is not exchanged. Gold and diamonds are valuable because a great deal of labour is required to find them, but virgin soil, the air and sunshine given by Nature have no value. "A thing can be a use-value, without having value."

It is in this sense that it is said that the *substance* of value is *abstract* human labour, independently of the skill and intensity or the particular kind of labour that goes into the production of a given individual commodity.

Section 2 is entitled the "Two-fold character of the labour embodied in commodities." Here Marx shows that the particular quality of labour, be that tailoring or brewing, corresponds to the use-value embodied in a commodity. However, just as a single person can divide their day between tailoring and brewing, the total social labour must be divided in whatever proportion is required to meet the total needs of the community. Therefore, in determining the quantity of labour embodied in a commodity, all that matters for the moment is the socially average labour time required for its production under existing conditions of production. Labour which is more skilled or more intense counts for the purpose of measuring its value only as "simple labour intensified," i.e., as a multiplied quantity of the same socially average labour. This is what is meant by "abstract labour." All labour in bourgeois society has both the character of the use-value it produces and the character of being a certain quantity of abstract labour.

If conditions of labour change so that one and the same coat can be produced in half the time, then the value of a coat is halved.

> An increase in the quantity of use values is an increase of material wealth. With two coats two men can be clothed, with one coat only one man. Nevertheless, an increased quantity of material wealth may correspond to a simultaneous fall in the magnitude of its value. This antagonistic movement has its origin in the two-fold character of labour.
>
> loc. cit.

This observation is worthy of emphasising: if a particular kind of labour is improved, for example by a technical innovation, then the quantity of wealth created may be increased, but its value is reduced! Thus, what Marx has disclosed within the commodity as a unit of value is a genuine contradiction: the *antagonism* between wealth-creating and value-creating.

Note that competition has not entered into consideration at all so far, and in fact, Marx's study of competition does not enter the picture until Chapter 10 of

Volume Three. Competition, though essential to capital, manifests itself only on the surface of economic life. Marx is effectively talking as if the community was one great enterprise dividing the labour time of its many independent producers between the production of various wanted commodities, and exchanging them at their value. If one party profits by cheating or clever bargaining, it is at the expense of the other party, and the *average* is not thereby affected.

Section 3 is entitled "The form of value or exchange value." Here Marx expresses the above contradiction as a commodity having *two forms*: the physical or natural form which makes it useful, and their value form. The remainder of this section is a quasi-historical exposition of the development of the value form from its beginning in an accidental trade between individuals up to the universal form, money.

I say *quasi*-historical because it is clearly an outcome of both Marx's study of relatively well-known facts about different historical forms of life and his logical inquisition of the commodity relation, what I have called a "categorical genealogy." This differs from the "real history" and is the same kind of logical-historical examination which Hegel used in the "Philosophy of Spirit." Here the sequence of categories is the same as the sequence found in history. Not the sequence of dominant relations in successive forms of life, but the succession of forms along one individual line of development.

I am not going to précis this rather long section, although it has been the focus of much interest from the point of view of identifying Hegelian categories. What Marx established here is the genesis of the form of value from the accidental form with one commodity emerging as a general measure of the value of all other commodities, to the universal form, the *money-form*, in which one commodity spontaneously singles itself out from all other commodities to act as the universal equivalent, expressing the relative value of all other commodities.

The historical narrative is broken off when this commodity has come to be gold. Gold is suitable for this role because of its extensive divisibility, its relative scarcity, its durability, its manifest purity, uniformity of quality and its specific weight. Thanks to the world market in gold, an ounce of gold represents a certain value, a certain quantity of abstract labour, and this value is to be the measure of all other products of labour of whatever type.

The value of money, i.e., gold, is not constant, but for example, will decline in the event of a gold rush bringing large amounts of relatively cheap gold on to the market, and fall again when new deposits of gold become scarce and require much labour to find and mine. All that remains constant is the unit of abstract labour time. Marx does discuss the value of bank-notes, but much later, in Volume Three, but he did not elaborate a theory of money as such, beyond this point.

Section 4 is entitled: "The fetishism of commodities and the secret thereof." This passage is not essential to the systematic exposition of forms of value in *Capital*, but was included because it sheds light on the nature of bourgeois ideology.

Marx likened the role of commodities (and *all* forms of value) in bourgeois society to fetishism, the belief held by religious people that material objects – icons, documents, buildings, and so on, have spiritual powers of their own that can control and intervene in human affairs.

> It is a definite social relation between men, that assumes, in their eyes, the fantastic form of a relation between things. In order, therefore, to find an analogy, we must have recourse to the mist-enveloped regions of the religious world. In that world the productions of the human brain appear as independent beings endowed with life, and entering into relation both with one another and the human race.
>
> loc. cit.

The social division of labour in bourgeois society means that people are collaborating in production with people with whom they have no personal contact. Thus, their own (collective) product assumes the appearance of a power independent and above them, and one, moreover, wielded by an alien class, and thus the appearance of being an alien power. This is in contrast to Hegel, who believed that the appearance of a worker's product on the market gave the worker some form of recognition. Hegel's blind spot was the result of conditions where the class antagonism between employers and employees had not developed and where the social division of labour was as yet undeveloped in Germany.

Despite this alienation, the notion of the moral equality of all human beings, the principle wielded against feudal privilege by the bourgeois revolution, finds its material basis in commodity production:

> The fact, that in the particular form of production with which we are dealing, viz., the production of commodities, the specific social character of private labour carried on independently, consists in the equality of every kind of that labour, by virtue of its being human labour, which character, therefore, assumes in the product the form of value
>
> loc. cit.

As a result of millions of such value-interactions every day, the notion of the equality of all human labour takes on the significance of an axiom. Universal suffrage has its origins in the universality of commodity production.

> The secret of the expression of value, namely, that all kinds of labour are equal and equivalent, because, and so far as they are human labour in general, cannot be deciphered, until the notion of human equality has already acquired the fixity of a popular prejudice. This, however, is possible only in a society in which the great mass of the produce of labour takes the form of commodities, in which, consequently, the dominant relation between man and man, is that of owners of commodities.
>
> op. cit.

1.1.2 Summary of *Capital*, Volume One, Chapter 1

The above synopsis hardly does justice to Marx's rich text, but my main point is to indicate where and how Marx is guided by or differs from Hegel, and to present the line of his argument in as clear terms as possible.

It is clear as daylight that Marx has followed Hegel's advice as set out in the first chapter of this book. His critique of Political Economy, culminating in his critique of Ricardo demonstrated that Political Economy was the division of science whose subject matter was essentially value, and that it was by the examination of value that the physiology of bourgeois society was to be revealed. As Hegel specified, value was to be analysed into all its parts and the simplest component part of value, given to everyday consciousness was to be chosen as the unit of value and made the starting point for analysis. Analysis of this unit must proceed initially without bringing it into relation with any other concept, revealing only what was contained within *it*.

The whole trajectory of Political Economy culminated in Ricardo's work and convinced Marx (if he was not already convinced) that it was indeed labour time which was the substance of value. Ricardo had failed to complete the task of reconstructing Political Economy on this basis because he had proceeded haphazardly, mixing up value with profit and price from the beginning before analysing the commodity form of value *in its own right*, abstracted from the historical conditions in which it is found in modernity. Marx makes only passing reference to price, noting that "exchange value *appears* to be something accidental."

Given that bourgeois society itself had historically grown out of commodity exchange through an historical passage across many different forms of society in which commodities and money played only a subordinate role underlines the importance of beginning, as Marx did, from analysis of the commodity.

Actual exchange of material commodities was as rare in Marx's times as it is today. The starting point was not determined empirically as the most common economic relation. If we were to take purchase and sale of services by electronic transfer as our starting point we would never get to the bottom of it all. Insofar as economic life has moved on since the 1860s, what is required is a *further development* of the analysis, but from this same starting point, analysis of the simplest economic relation between people, the commodity.

In this chapter, Marx considered only the production and exchange of commodities at their value. Wage labour and capital are not yet examined. The chapter thus represents an analytical abstraction in which many independent producers (artisans and agricultural labourers) exchange their own produce and are paid, as Marx notes in §4, according to their labour time. This analytical abstraction is an image of the petit-bourgeois ideal, like the kind of society envisioned by the French anarchist and contemporary of Marx, Pierre-Joseph Proudhon. It is the first of a series of such universal conceptions which will be layered each upon those which have gone before to reconstruct the modern capitalist economy in conceptual form.

The contradiction which Marx uncovered in the commodity relation is the beginning of the analysis but by no means the end. It is wrong to suggest as others have that the entirety of *Capital* is based simply on the analysis of the commodity. As we noted in our brief review of Marx's critique of Ricardo, a number of problems remained to be solved, and in each case these problems would become the focus of *new* insights and new divisions of the subject matter each beginning with their own prius.

Nonetheless, the fundamental antagonism between wealth and value which Marx discovered within the commodity runs right through bourgeois society in general and capitalism in particular, encapsulating as it does the fundamental antagonism between the capitalist mode of exploitation and the developing forces of production, that is, the labour process itself.

1.1.3 Chapter 2. Exchange

The opening lines of Chapter 2 are a précis of the early sections of Hegel's *Philosophy of Right*, in which property originates in first possession, objectifying a person's will in personal property, and exchange entailing mutual recognition and constituting a contract based on mutual consent. However, Marx argued that it is the act of *exchange* which is the first judicial (i.e., genuinely human) relation, rather than simply private *property*, as it was for Hegel.

> The persons exist for one another merely as representatives of, and, therefore. as owners of, commodities. In the course of our investigation

> we shall find, in general, that the characters who appear on the economic stage are but the personifications of the economic relations that exist between them.
>
> MARX, 1867, Chapter 2

It is the act of exchange which realises the exchange value and proves that the commodity does indeed contain a use-value. Marx says that the act of exchange is simultaneously private (in that it realises the wants of each party) and social, in that the establishment of the exchange value and its use-value is a social act, in fact, with implications across the entire community. In this way Marx continued the logical-historical narrative from §3 of Chapter 1 ("The intermediate steps of the process vanish in the result and leave no trace behind"), and shows how beginning with accidental acts of exchange, one commodity must emerge as the universal equivalent, money, which separates itself from all other commodities.

Money is a commodity, albeit a special commodity. But if one had started with money alongside the commodity, rather than starting with the commodity alone, then the nature of money would have remained mysterious.

1.1.4 Chapter 3. Money

In this section, Marx reviews the various functions of money which had emerged historically, but from the character of money as the universal equivalent commodity money is: the measure of values, the medium of circulation, a hoard, a symbol of value, the means of payment and universal, i.e., worldwide money, acting as a national reserve, and facilitating exchange between countries even in times of crisis.

This ends Part I of *Capital* Volume One.

1.1.5 Summary of Part I

Marx's division of *Capital* into *parts* is significant. The first six parts of *Capital* begin with a simple form of value which functions as the prius or germ cell for the development which follows. Generally, each part marks a division of the subject matter in the sense in which divisions are to be made in Hegel's "Idea of the True." Parts VII and VIII of Volume One depart from this strict logical narrative, allowing Marx to examine historical aspects of the subject matter and miscellanea. In the second volume, this division into parts is retained right to the end. Only Parts VII and VIII of Volume One and Part VII of Volume Three are extraneous to the logical structure of *Capital*.

In this Part I, Marx has established the concept of "value" in its simplest form, commodities, and Marx proceeds by means of an analysis of the commodity, identifying its internal contradiction – the conflict between use-value and exchange-value. He demonstrates that money, the subject of endless confusion and mysticism, is a *type of commodity*, and subject to the nature of commodities. At this point money is taken to be gold. The particular nature of paper money and other varieties of currency is left to later stages in the development in Volume Three.

All other forms of value lie ahead and must be synthesised from the concept of value so far established.

Moreover, the society of independent producers exchanging their products at their value, bourgeois society, as outlined in Part I is an analytical abstraction. But at the same it is a certain *viable form of life* governed by the ideal of the mutual independence and equality of all human beings. It arose historically among the independent artisans and merchants in mediaeval times, who exchanged their products at their value and made collective decisions on the basis of one man one vote. The economic law established in Part I is also an ethical norm, specifically the ethical norm carried by the bourgeois revolution.

1.2 *Part II. The Transformation of Money into Capital*

1.2.1 Chapter 4. The General Formula for Capital

> The circulation of commodities is the starting-point of capital. The production of commodities, their circulation, and that more developed form of their circulation called commerce, these form the historical groundwork from which it rises. ...
>
> As a matter of history, capital, as opposed to landed property, invariably takes the form at first of money; it appears as moneyed wealth, as the capital of the merchant and of the usurer. ... All new capital, to commence with, comes on the stage, that is, on the market, whether of commodities, labour, or money, even in our days, in the shape of money that by a definite process has to be transformed into capital.
>
> The first distinction we notice between money that is money only, and money that is capital, is nothing more than a difference in their form of circulation.
>
> MARX, Chapter 4, 1867

Following the method demonstrated by Hegel in his *Logic*, it can be seen that Marx has established that value in the circulation of commodities and the formation of money are the logical, historical and immediate preconditions of capital. On this basis alone, Marx is able to introduce a novel definition of capital: *buying in order to sell* (M–C–M) instead of selling in order to buy (C–M–C) which is characteristic of the form of society presupposed in Part I.

That this activity arises from the circulation of commodities mediated by money is clear. To this very day, capital remains money which is put into circulation to be withdrawn again, "buying in order to sell." Marx defined capital solely in terms of the concepts already established: value, commodities, circulation and money. As a result, Marx has been able to define *capital in general* – be it industrial capital or merchant capital, but distinguished, for example, from traditional landed property which is not subject to circulation as a commodity at all. (Land which is bought and sold as a commodity is land which has been transformed into bourgeois property and is no longer traditional landed property). As Hegel demanded, Marx moves from the general to the particular. But first he must define *universal capital* – that individual form of capital which exists alongside other forms of capital, but which is universal, universal (*allgemeine*) because all particular forms of capital must be seen as modifications of this universal form.

The circuit (C–M–C) ends with a different commodity than that with which it began and each cycle proceeds independently of the previous cycle in response to a new need. On the other hand, (M–C–M) ends with the same commodity it began with, namely money. This would be absurd and inexplicable, unless the circuit ends with an *expanded* sum of money, M' or M + ΔM.

> This increment or excess over the original value I call "surplus-value." The value originally advanced, therefore, not only remains intact while in circulation, but adds to itself a surplus-value or expands itself. It is this movement that converts it into capital.
>
> op. cit.

Money in circulation is only *potential* capital.

Whereas the person who sells in order to buy will be satisfied with the commodity they have acquired and will begin a new cycle only when stimulated by a new need, the buyer who aims to recover their money completes the cycle with an expanded sum of the same money ready to repeat the same cycle in an expanded form. "Money ends the movement only to begin it again. ... The circulation of capital has therefore no limits."

> Because [capital] is value, it has acquired the occult quality of being able to add value to itself. It brings forth living offspring, or, at the least, lays golden eggs.
>
> op. cit.

Marx makes clear that the person who buys in order to sell dearer is nothing but the personification of an economic category.

> As the conscious representative of this movement, the possessor of money becomes a capitalist. His person, or rather his pocket, is the point from which the money starts and to which it returns. ... he functions as a capitalist, that is, as capital personified and endowed with consciousness and a will.
>
> op. cit.

Note that capital is distinguished above all by the mode of its circulation; a hoard is not capital. "While the miser is merely a capitalist gone mad, the capitalist is a rational miser."

Incidentally, Marx has also defined "surplus value," ΔM, but has not yet identified its *source*.

1.2.2 Chapter 5. Contradictions in the General Formula of Capital

Despite the illusions of the bourgeoisie, surplus value cannot arise from the circulation of money, exchanging commodities at their value, with or without the medium of money. If a commodity is sold above its value, and thereby the buyer makes a gain, this is only by swindling the buyer, who has lost just as much as the seller gained. No new value is created by swindling or by smart trading.

It is only by buying in order to sell more dearly that surplus value can be extracted. This is the first step in the solution of the foremost problem of political economy: the source of surplus value.

The merchant "parasitically shoves" themself between seller and buyer, and there are a myriad of ways in which the merchant can see to it that he makes a gain at the cost to his supplier or his customer. Likewise, the usurer makes a profit, but only thanks to the loss on the part of their debtors.

Although merchant's capital and usurer's capital are "derivative forms" of capital, "these two forms appear in the course of history before the modern standard form of capital." History runs counter to logic in this instance.

Since surplus value cannot be created in circulation, "something must take place in the background, which is not apparent in the circulation itself." The capitalist could add the value of his own labour, but this does not explain the "self-expanding value" which is what is at issue.

The surplus appears to originate "both in circulation, but yet not in circulation."

With this Marx now names the *embryo* of capital, the *prius* – germ cell or universal individual, which at this embryonic moment is literally a person, whom Marx calls "Moneybags."

> Our friend, Moneybags, who as yet is only an embryo capitalist, must buy his commodities at their value, must sell them at their value, and yet at the end of the process must withdraw more value from circulation than he threw into it at starting. His development into a full-grown capitalist must take place, both within the sphere of circulation and without it. These are the conditions of the problem.
>
> loc. cit.

From the point of view of understanding the Hegelian roots of *Capital* it is vital to grasp this moment. Just as in the first Preface to *Capital*, Marx referred to the commodity as the "economic cell form" of value, explicitly alluding to Hegel's *der Keim* (seed), he again explicitly alludes to *der Keim*, this time as an *embryo* (*Schmetterlingsentfaltung*, literally the larva of a butterfly), marking the starting point of a *new division* of science.

It is wrong to see the commodity form of value as the germ cell of *capitalism*. The germ cell of value, yes, and thus the germ cell of bourgeois society and the ethos of the moral equality of all people. But the arrival of Moneybags is a *new departure*, and sets in train the development of a new phenomenon.

As the germ cell of the unit of capital, the capitalist firm, Moneybags is just as significant as the commodity itself. The simplest unit of universal capital.

1.2.3 Chapter 6. The Buying and Selling of Labour-Power

This chapter addresses an outstanding problem in Political Economy, the *source of surplus value*, highlighted by the contradiction Marx has identified in capital: surplus value can appear neither in circulation nor outside of circulation, but only in the process of putting money into circulation and then withdrawing money from circulation.

Marx finds the solution to this problem by focusing on the buying and selling of *one* commodity amongst all others, labour-power (just as he defined value by focusing on *one* form of value amongst others, the commodity). Marx said the Political Economists had failed to grasp the particular nature of the labour found in the capitalist economy which Marx has described as "abstract labour." Now he makes a further analysis of the nature of this abstract labour.

The Political Economists had already determined that the value of labour-power was determined by the cost of the means of subsistence of a labourer.

However, the Political Economists had made no distinction between living labour, consumed by the capitalist, and labour power – the commodity purchased on the market at its value and *used* by the capitalist, under his direction, with his tools and on his materials.

> In order that he [the worker] may be able to do this, he must have it at his disposal, must be the untrammelled owner of his capacity for labour, i.e., of his person. He and the owner of money meet in the market, and deal with each other as on the basis of equal rights, with this difference alone, that one is buyer, the other seller; both, therefore, equal in the eyes of the law. The continuance of this relation demands that the owner of the labour-power should sell it only for a definite period, for if he were to sell it rump and stump, once for all, he would be selling himself, converting himself from a free man into a slave, from an owner of a commodity into a commodity.
>
> MARX, 1867, Chapter 6

Without distinguishing between living labour and labour power, the source of surplus value remained mysterious, leading to all kinds of magical thinking and logical gymnastics.

This contradiction within the concept of "labour" as both the application of "labour power" and "living labour" completes Part II on the essential nature of modern industrial capital. Usurers and merchant capitalists were merely undeveloped forms of capital, which creamed off a share of the surplus from an existing labour process. They are now relegated to the status of *particular* and inessential forms of capital, which seize a portion of the value circulating in the market, but without participating in its creation in the labour process. Industrial capital, on the other hand, takes over and uses the labour process for its own ends, by the buying and consumption of labour power. Industrial capital is the universal form of capital.

In an unpublished Chapter 6 of *Capital*, Marx (1864) identifies a precursor to industrial capital in which the capitalist merely gathers a number of workers together in a single workshop and extracts their surplus value, but without transforming the nature of the labour. It was industrial capital proper which transformed this artisanal labour into factory labour. This intermediate stage in the historical development of capitalism was omitted in the final draft of *Capital*.

In outlining this process, Marx points to the social and historical conditions that are necessary for the capitalist to be able to buy "free" labour-power at its value and realise the value of the product on the market. Such an activity is incompatible with the conditions presupposed in Part I in which the labourers were all independent producers who owned their own means of production and were in command of their own labour. Before the conditions described in Part II could flourish, the labourers had to be deprived of their means of production.

> Capital, therefore, announces from its first appearance a new epoch in the process of social production.
>
> loc. cit.

The value of labour-power, dependent on the cost of the means of subsistence of a worker, differs somewhat from the value of other commodities however.

> His means of subsistence must therefore be sufficient to maintain him in his normal state as a labouring individual. His natural wants, such as food, clothing, fuel, and housing, vary according to the climatic and other physical conditions of his country. On the other hand, the number and extent of his so-called necessary wants, as also the modes of satisfying them, are themselves the product of historical development, and depend therefore to a great extent on the degree of civilisation of a country, more particularly on the conditions under which, and consequently on the habits and degree of comfort in which, the class of free labourers has been formed. In contradistinction therefore to the case of other commodities, there enters into the determination of the value of labour-power a historical and moral element.
>
> loc. cit.

Not only does the cost of labour-power include the cost of the worker's physical needs, but also the cost of raising the next generation of workers, and their education as demanded by the modern labour process.

> Accompanied by Mr. Moneybags and by the possessor of labour-power, we therefore take leave for a time of this noisy sphere, where everything takes place on the surface and in view of all men, and follow them both into the hidden abode of production, on whose threshold there stares us in the face "No admittance except on business." Here we shall see, not only how capital produces, but how capital is produced. We shall at last force the secret of profit making. ...
>
> He, who before was the money-owner, now strides in front as capitalist; the possessor of labour-power follows as his labourer. The one with

> an air of importance, smirking, intent on business; the other, timid and holding back, like one who is bringing his own hide to market and has nothing to expect but – a hiding.
>
> loc. cit.

1.2.4 Summary of Part II

Part II is a *distinct division of the subject matter.* In Part I, the germ cell of value was the commodity; in Part II, the germ cell of capital (Mr. Moneybags) is the unit of capital, the single capitalist firm. The embryo of capital is a new prius, which can emerge from the process of circulation of commodities once money participates in circulation.

The ethical life presupposed in Part I is a society of independent producers exchanging their products at value; the ethical life of Part II is a society in which "free" (free also of means of production) labourers sell their labour-power on the market to units of capital which consume that labour-power as living labour applied to means of production which is the private property of the capitalist. *The independent capitalist producer has now replaced the independent artisan* but is still in its embryonic form as the single entrepreneur. Like the artisans of Part I, these agents exchange their products at their value.

Part II was made possible by analysis of the kind of labour that arises in a community in which capital has appeared; "labour" as it had been understood by the Political Economists was both "labour-power," the capacity to labour whose value depends on the worker's cost of living, *and* "living labour," engaged with the capitalist's means of production and the very substance of value itself.

At this point, it remains the case that we have a society made of independent producers selling their products at their value. Surplus value in the form of profit arises because the value of the ingredients of the labour process is less than the value of its product.

Marx has identified the site of production of surplus value, but has yet to reveal *how* this surplus value arises and what determines its *magnitude*. This is the outstanding contradiction, the aporia in Part II.

The progress of Marx's critique of the science of value is proceeding exactly as per Hegel's advice in The *Logic* – identifying a unit, analysing that unit, and identifying problems or contradictions which arise from analysis without the introduction of any new material. At each stage of the reconstruction we find a viable way of life with its own characteristic ethos, even if its description is incomplete and even though it may never have been an historically dominant form of state.

1.3 *Part III. The Production of Absolute Surplus-Value*

1.3.1 Chapter 7. The Labour-Process & Process of Producing Surplus-Value

In §1 of this chapter Marx presents an analysis of the labour process as characteristic of human life at all stages of its historical development:

> Labour is, in the first place, a process in which both man and Nature participate, and in which man of his own accord starts, regulates, and controls the material re-actions between himself and Nature. He opposes himself to Nature as one of her own forces, setting in motion arms and legs, head and hands, the natural forces of his body, in order to appropriate Nature's productions in a form adapted to his own wants. By thus acting on the external world and changing it, he at the same time changes his own nature.
>
> ... The labour-process, resolved as above into its simple elementary factors, is human action with a view to the production of use-values, ... it is the everlasting Nature-imposed condition of human existence, and therefore is independent of every social phase of that existence, or rather, is common to every such phase.
>
> MARX, 1867, Chapter 7

The analysis is interesting in itself but functions merely to set the scene for §2 which must address the contradiction identified in Part II, the production of surplus value in the use of labour-power. Marx notes the two facts which distinguish the labour process as it exists under capital from the general nature of labour common to all social formations. "The labour-process, turned into the process by which the capitalist consumes labour-power, exhibits two characteristic phenomena":

> First, the labourer works under the control of the capitalist

and

> Secondly, the product is the property of the capitalist and not that of the labourer, its immediate producer. ... From the instant he steps into the workshop, the use-value of his labour-power, and therefore also its use, which is labour, belongs to the capitalist. By the purchase of labour-power, the capitalist incorporates labour, as a living ferment, with the lifeless constituents of the product. From his point of view, the labour-process

> is nothing more than the consumption of the commodity purchased, *i.e.*, of labour-power.
>
> op. cit.

In Part II, Marx had already shown that *this* is the site at which surplus value is produced, and it remains now to show *how* this is possible in a society in which all commodities are exchanged at their value.

1.3.2 §2. The Production of Surplus Value

Marx shows that the value of the product is the sum total of the value of the materials *transformed* in production of each product and the proportion of the value of the machinery necessary to be *used up* in the production of each product plus the labour-time (the number of days of abstract or average labour) *consumed* in the production of the product.

The value of one day's labour-power (*i.e.* the value of the necessities of life daily required on average by the labourer) will be embodied in the product after a certain number of hours. That is, after a certain number of hours, say eight hours, the worker has produced *the equivalent of one day's labour-power*, their day's wage. Once the capitalist has sold the product at its value and paid the worker their wage, both the capitalist and the worker have recovered their costs, *i.e.*, the value of their contribution to the production of the product.

However, the capitalist entered into the bargain and paid the worker for the use of their labour-power with the hope of getting something for his "service" in providing access to his means of production, but at this point the labourer is ready to go home, having met his needs for the day. Before Mr. Moneybags had entered the picture, that is exactly what the worker (or journeyman) would probably do: go home.

However,

> What really influenced [the capitalist] was the specific use-value which this commodity possesses of being *a source not only of value, but of more value than it has itself.* This is the special service that the capitalist expects from labour-power.
>
> op. cit.

The capitalist forces the worker to continue working for the *rest of the day*, but does not pay the labourer for these additional hours. The capitalist is the owner of the entire product of say, 12 hours' exercise of labour-power, and therefore on sale of the product will realise the value, not only of the ingredients purchased for the production of the commodity, but as well of, say, 4 hours of unpaid labour.

> The process of production, considered on the one hand as the unity of the labour-process and the process of creating value, is production of commodities; considered on the other hand as the unity of the labour-process and the process of producing surplus-value, it is the capitalist process of production, or capitalist production of commodities.
>
> op. cit.

The quantity of surplus value appropriated by the capitalist each day is equal to the number hours of unpaid labour forced out of the worker each day. The capitalist pays only for the number of hours labour socially necessary for the reproduction of the worker's energy, at the present stage of development of the labour process this is less than the number of hours actually worked.

1.3.3 Conclusion from Chapter 7

Marx lays a lot of irony and polemics on to this passage, but the essence is clear. The source of surplus value is the labour-time worked over and above that which is socially necessary for the reproduction of the worker's own life, appropriated as part of the entire product, surplus labour-time. This *unpaid labour-time* is surplus value.

The problem set at the end of Part II is now resolved into the question of unpaid labour time, essentially, the excessive length of the working day. The enormous importance of this discovery lies in the fact that the length of the working day is something which is within the practical reach of the industrial workers' movement. In 1856, in Melbourne, the international 8-hour Movement had been launched, and the struggle to reduce the length of the working day has now been shown to be the substance of the exploitation of the working class by capital through *unpaid labour-time*. An immensely practical discovery!

Unpaid labour time is the germ cell from which grows the exploitation of the working class by capital. It's not a "combination of factors," just unpaid labour time.

The error that the Political Economists had made in being unable to see how this surplus labour-time is exploited was their failure to distinguish between *labour-power* – the product which the worker sells to the capitalist for their use, and living *labour* manifested once the labourer is put to work at the will of the capitalist.

The rest of Part III must now examine unpaid labour time, and how both the rate and mass of surplus value acquired by capital develops from this germ cell.

1.3.4 Chapter 8. Constant Capital and Variable Capital

Marx criticised Ricardo for failing to distinguish between profit (on capital) and surplus value (extracted from the employment of wage labour). To do this, Marx analysed the unit of capital into its component parts.

> The labourer adds fresh value to the subject of his labour by expending upon it a given amount of additional labour, no matter what the specific character and utility of that labour may be. On the other hand, the values of the means of production used up in the process are preserved, and present themselves afresh as constituent parts of the value of the product; the values of the cotton and the spindle, for instance, re-appear again in the value of the yarn. The value of the means of production is therefore preserved, by being transferred to the product. ...
>
> By the simple addition of a certain quantity of labour, new value is added, and by the quality of this added labour, the original values of the means of production are preserved in the product.
>
> MARX, 1867, Chapter 8

The value of the means of production, both the material transformed and the machinery used up, *reappears* in the value of the product, unchanged in its magnitude by the transformation in its form brought about by labour, the application of labour-power. This Marx calls "constant capital."

> That part of capital then, which is represented by the means of production, by the raw material, auxiliary material and the instruments of labour does not, in the process of production, undergo any quantitative alteration of value. I therefore call it the constant part of capital, or, more shortly, *constant capital.*

Whilst

> that part of capital, represented by labour-power, does, in the process of production, undergo an alteration of value. It both reproduces the equivalent of its own value, and also produces an excess, a surplus-value, which may itself vary, may be more or less according to circumstances. This part of capital is continually being transformed from a constant into a variable magnitude. I therefore call it the variable part of capital, or, shortly, *variable capital.*
>
> op. cit.

Constant capital and variable capital are new and crucial concepts, but Marx does not endow them with a new "Part" in the structure of *Capital*, because they are derivatives of the units he has already derived – capital, surplus value and unpaid labour-time.

Throughout this chapter Marx repeatedly emphasises that the specific quality of the labour-power applied in the production process, be that spinning or tailoring, is irrelevant to the quantities of value embodied in the product. This analysis is equally applicable to *all* commodity production, dependent only on quantities of abstract labour. It is in the nature of modern industrial capital that all kinds of labour, of whatever trade, are interchangeable with one another in the labour market.

This analysis of the unit of capital into three components: constant capital, variable capital (i.e., wages) and surplus labour-time is the key to Marx's distinction between profit and surplus value.

1.3.5 Chapter 9. The Rate of Surplus-Value

This chapter is divided into four sections, each devoted to different aspects of surplus value and its substance, surplus labour-time.

§1 is entitled "The degree of exploitation of labour-power."

> The relative quantity produced, or the increase per cent of the variable capital, is determined, it is plain, by the ratio of the surplus-value (s) to the variable capital (v), or is expressed by s/v. ... This relative increase in the value of the variable capital, or the relative magnitude of the surplus-value, I call, "the rate of surplus-value."
>
> MARX, 1867, Chapter 9

The proportion of the time the worker needs to reproduce the equivalent of her wage is called the "necessary" labour time; during the second period of the working day which is no longer necessary for the labourer, and produces no value for herself, "and to the labour expended during that time, I give the name of surplus-labour."

> The rate of surplus-value is therefore an exact expression for the degree of exploitation of labour-power by capital, or of the labourer by the capitalist.
>
> loc. cit.

§2 makes the point that as the value of the product is so divided that the product itself is likewise divided between constant capital, labour necessary for the reproduction of the worker's own life and surplus labour, which the capitalist converts into money.

Both these sections are filled out with interminable examples of how these quantities are realised and divided between capitalist and worker.

§3 is entitled "Senior's last hour," and pours scorn on the Political Economist Nassau Senior who in 1836 expressed outrage at the newly passed Factory Act and "the still more menacing Ten-hours' agitation." Marx simply making the point of how conscious the bourgeoisie was of the value of the unpaid labour time.

§4 on "Surplus produce" emphasises again that the surplus value and surplus product is properly measured against the *necessary* labour time:

> The sum of the necessary labour and the surplus-labour, *i.e.*, of the periods of time during which the workman replaces the value of his labour-power, and produces the surplus-value, this sum constitutes the actual time during which he works, *i.e.*, the working-day.
>
> loc. cit.

1.3.6 Chapter 10. The Working Day

This chapter is 34,000 words occupying 10% of Volume One of *Capital*. It adds little to the logical derivation of Marx's critique of political economy. However, it is crammed with empirical data documenting the horrific practices of the British industrial capitalists and the mighty struggle of the nascent workers' movement against the excessive length of the working day. The chapter makes it abundantly clear that Marx believes that this issue, specifically the Ten Hours Movement, is the central struggle against capitalist exploitation. There is, on the other hand, very little to be found in *Capital* on the wages struggle, far less the Socialist movement's struggle against capital as a whole.

Where one of the findings of *Capital* has great significance for the struggle of the working class, we see Marx elaborating the topic far in excess of what is needed for the logical argument, clearly intending it as an intervention in the struggle itself.

1.3.7 Chapter 11. The Rate and Mass of Surplus-Value

Here Marx shows that the total mass of surplus value extracted from workers by one unit of capital per working day is equal to the *rate of exploitation* times the number of workers employed. This rate of exploitation is the same whether computed in terms surplus as a proportion to wages, or the ratio of unpaid labour time to necessary labour time.

It is always supposed that the value of an average labour-power is constant, or at least beyond the control of the individual capitalist. By nature, there is an absolute limit to the length of the working day (24 hours), so the only means an individual capitalist has of increasing the mass of surplus product or value obtained is to employ more workers. Given average workers and products sold at their value, the only way a capital can increase the share of surplus value they can lay hands on is by increasing his expenditure on wages or extending the working day. The amount of material used up in production has no effect on the amount of surplus value obtained. In any given community, a labourer's cost of subsistence is the same wherever she may be employed, and the length of the working day is either legislated or set by custom, so it follows that whatever trade a capitalist may be engaged in (in a given country), the rate of surplus value will be the same, all else being equal.

Here Marx draws attention to the fact that in different trades (Marx compares spinning cotton and baking bread) the amount of constant capital consumed in the product of each day's labour varies widely, and yet:

> This law clearly contradicts all experience based on appearance. Everyone knows that a cotton spinner, who, reckoning the percentage on the whole of his applied capital, employs much constant and little variable capital, does not, on account of this, pocket less profit or surplus-value than a baker, who relatively sets in motion much variable and little constant capital. For the solution of this apparent contradiction, many intermediate terms are as yet wanted
>
> loc. cit. Chapter 11

This is the first mention of the "stumbling block" on which Ricardo came to grief. Ricardo had written into Chapter 1 of his book the empirical fact that the rate of profit is universal and the value of labour time, and therefore the rate of surplus value, is also universal. Note that Marx characterised the independence of the profitability of capital and the proportion spent on wages as an "appearance" resulting in an "apparent contradiction."

Nonetheless, Ricardo had failed to observe, as Marx has shown, that these two data are in flagrant contradiction.

> The labour which is set in motion by the total capital of a society, day in, day out, may be regarded as a single collective working day. ... With a given length of this working day, whether its limits are fixed physically or socially, the mass of surplus-value can only be increased by increasing the number of labourers, *i.e.*, of the labouring population, [but] by the

> possible lengthening of the working day. It will, however, be seen in the following chapter that this law only holds for the form of surplus-value dealt with up to the present.
>
> loc. cit.

Here Marx stops to dwell on how it is that Mr. Moneybags has entered into this situation. He points out that in order to produce surplus value a certain sum of money must be in the hands of an individual, enough to cover, Marx reckons, the wages of one worker for a year and buy sufficient means of production. But in this event, Mr. Moneybags would be able to live only at a fraction of the level of a common labourer (presuming that the rate of exploitation is less than 100%), and consequently enough money for the wages and means production for a year's work by at least several labourers is necessary before you can get into this game. "A certain stage of capitalist production necessitates that the capitalist be able to devote the whole of the time during which he functions as a capitalist, i.e., as personified capital, to the appropriation and therefore control of the labour of others, and to the selling of the products of this labour." And Marx observes that:

> The guilds of the middle ages therefore tried to prevent by force the transformation of the master of a trade into a capitalist, by limiting the number of labourers that could be employed by one master within a very small maximum. The possessor of money or commodities actually turns into a capitalist in such cases only where the minimum sum advanced for production greatly exceeds the maximum of the middle ages.
>
> loc. cit.

The sum of money necessary to transform oneself into a capitalist varies from one trade to another but historically it is continuously increasing with the development of the technique.

Over time, capital took on an increasingly coercive character so as to compel workers to do more work than their way of living required. The character of the productive process changed so as to absorb increasing numbers of workers, and the capitalist intervenes in social life in every way possible in order to compel "free" labourers to enter his factory.

1.3.8 Summary of Part III

Part III is again a *new division of the subject matter* of political economy.

Part II had identified the employment of labour-power by a capitalist as the site of production of surplus value, so Part III had to analyse the labour process as it is found in capitalism to reveal how surplus value is realised in this process. To do this Marx identified a *new* germ cell, *unpaid labour time*. Unpaid labour time is not inherent in commodity production. Indeed, commodity production had existed for centuries alongside forced labour for the benefit of landed property, and participation in artisan or commercial workshops was a way to *escape* forced labour. Indeed, in pre-capitalist literature it was customary to refer to wage-labourers as "independent" in contradistinction to servants and peasants who were "dependent" (Fraser & Gordon, 1990).

Unpaid labour time was a *new* insight reflecting a new element which had entered the labour process with the transformation of the mediaeval guild master into a capitalist, a new germ cell.

Marx then proceeded to analyse this new unit, still under conditions of commodities being sold at their value and on the assumption, consistent with the concept of "abstract labour," that all workers share much the same conditions of life, gaining their subsistence from like sources such that their labour power is sold at an average prices and affords an average subsistence standard of living according to the customs and practices of the day.

The unit of unpaid labour-time corresponds to the division of value into constant capital (passed in unchanged quantity from the means of production into the product), variable capital (the total wage bill) and surplus value corresponding to the unpaid labour time.

This leads Marx to consideration of the (length of the) working day, clearly signalled by Marx as the central bone of contention between worker and capitalist. It is as a result of this conflict that capital had broken out of the constraints of the mediaeval guild and now shamelessly forced the proletarian to work as many hours as can be found in the day in order to appropriate unpaid labour time. At the same time, Mr. Moneybags has shed his chrysalis and taken flight as the fully fledged industrial capitalist.

At this moment Marx can point to the contradiction between the social norms in which commodities are exchanged at their value and concomitantly, the capitalist appropriating surplus according to a socially average rate of surplus value, and the well-known empirical fact that the capitalist enjoys a uniform *socially average rate of profit* of capital invested, *irrespective* of the proportion of that capital which is invested in wages and was therefore the source of the unpaid labour, which is the substance of the surplus product acquired.

> For the solution of this apparent contradiction, many intermediate terms are as yet wanted.
>
> op. cit.

In fact, the reader must wait till Part II of Volume Three for this contradiction to be resolved. In the meantime, Marx must analyse surplus labour time and discover the determinants of its magnitude – which is after all, essential to capitalist development.

The form of society presupposed by Part IV, one in which impoverished proletarians are forced to work excessively long hours in the factory is aptly encapsulated by "unpaid labour." The contradiction here lies in the fact that the capitalist comes up against an immovable barrier – there are only so many hours in a day and a worker cannot live on thin air alone.

1.4 *Part IV. The Production of Relative Surplus-Value*

1.4.1 Chapter 12. The Concept of Relative Surplus-Value

Marx had already referred to surplus-value as "absolute surplus value" without defining what was meant by "absolute." Unpaid labour time is the difference between the length of the working day and the necessary labour time, both of which appear to be constrained by absolute limits.

This is the problem which must be resolved in Part Four – the *necessary labour time* is the new unit/germ cell to be analysed, but in the shape of "relative surplus value."

Just as Ricardo and the other Political Economists had treated the value of wages as a fixed quantity being the subsistence level of the average worker, Marx has also up to this point taken the necessary labour time as a given datum. Certainly there is nothing an individual capitalist can do about the magnitude of necessary labour time of the workers he employs; if he pays the worker any less, the worker will not be able to live or work.

In the earliest phase of capitalist development, a master would simply gather as many workers as he could into a workshop, work them as long as possible and reap profit from their unpaid labour. The constant pressure to increase the productivity of their employees by investing in technique failed to lead to increased profit, as was shown in Part III. This contradiction unleashed a new tendency in capitalism – the drive to revolutionise the means of production which is characteristic of industrial capitalism. (See "The Direct Process of Production," the "unpublished draft Sixth Chapter of *Capital*," Marx 1864).

> a fall in the value of labour-power implies, however, that the same necessaries of life which were formerly produced in ten hours, can now be produced in nine hours. But this is impossible without an increase in the productiveness of labour. … an alteration in the labour-process, of

> such a kind as to shorten the labour-time socially necessary for the production of a commodity. ... The technical and social conditions of the process, and consequently the very mode of production must be revolutionised, before the productiveness of labour can be increased. By that means alone can the value of labour-power be made to sink, and the portion of the working day necessary for the reproduction of that value, be shortened.
>
> MARX, 1867, Chapter 12

The individual capitalist can do nothing to reduce the necessary labour time (and thereby expand the unpaid labour time) of his own employees. But *collectively*, as a result of their shared activity in reducing the costs of production of each use-value by the use of machinery, the lower cost of producing the use-values which constitute the necessary labour of their own employees leads to a gradual reduction in necessary labour time. It is in particular the cost of production of those products which constitute the basic needs of working people which has the effect of reducing necessary labour time. This takes place despite the lack of interest of any individual capitalist in reducing the cost of living for working people.

> The shortening of the working day is, therefore, by no means what is aimed at, in capitalist production, when labour is economised by increasing its productiveness.
>
> op. cit.

The addition to unpaid labour achieved by reduction of the value of wages is called *relative surplus value*, relative because it is achieved by changing the proportions into which the working day is divided, rather than by simply adding unpaid labour time. Further,

> But the value of a commodity is determined, not only by the quantity of labour which the labourer directly bestows upon that commodity, but also by the labour contained in the means of production. ... Hence, a fall in the value of labour-power is also brought about by an increase in the productiveness of labour, and by a corresponding cheapening of commodities in those industries which supply the instruments of labour and the raw material, that form the material elements of the constant capital required for producing the necessaries of life.
>
> op. cit.

This latter effect tends to reduce the constant capital component of the value of a commodity at the same time that the component of variable capital is reduced by the same process. As a result, the capitalists' rate of profit fails to enjoy the increase that the capitalist desires, but the revolutionising of the labour process and the resulting cheapening of labour-power and the increase in the rate of exploitation is a secular historical tendency.

1.4.2 Chapter 13. Co-operation

As alluded to earlier, a revolution in the capitalist development of the labour process takes place as a result of capitalists' efforts to reduce the necessary labour time embodied in their products

> Capitalist production only then really begins, as we have already seen, when each individual capital employs simultaneously a comparatively large number of labourers; when consequently the labour-process is carried on on an extensive scale and yields, relatively, large quantities of products. A greater number of labourers working together, at the same time, in one place (or, if you will, in the same field of labour), in order to produce the same sort of commodity under the mastership of one capitalist, constitutes, both historically and logically, the starting-point of capitalist production. With regard to the mode of production itself, manufacture, in its strict meaning, is hardly to be distinguished, in its earliest stages, from the handicraft trades of the guilds, otherwise than by the greater number of workmen simultaneously employed by one and the same individual capital. The workshop of the medieval master handicraftsman is simply enlarged.
>
> MARX, 1867, Chapter 13

The employment of large numbers of workers makes the differences between one or another worker irrelevant; labour more and more resembles the "abstract labour" implicit in capitalist development. Moreover, in these large enterprises, it is no longer the case that each product is the work of one employee, for the product has passed through many hands in the process of production and each person's labour is but an "aliquot part" of the necessary labour of the product.

> Thus the laws of the production of value are only fully realised for the individual producer, when he produces as a capitalist, and employs a number of workmen together, whose labour, by its collective nature, is at once stamped as average social labour.
>
> op. cit.

The *principles* implicit in bourgeois society laid out in earlier chapters have now become the *actuality* of capitalist production. Marx remarks:

> The march of our analysis compels this splitting up of the subject-matter, a splitting up that is quite in keeping with the spirit of capitalist production.
>
> op. cit.

Capital now makes use not only of the economies of size but also the power of cooperative labour. As a result, the concentration of large masses of workers together becomes a pre-condition for participation in the production process, and:

> The work of directing, superintending, and adjusting, becomes one of the functions of capital, from the moment that the labour under the control of capital, becomes co-operative. ... An industrial army of workmen, under the command of a capitalist, requires, like a real army, officers (managers), and sergeants (foremen, overlookers), who, while the work is being done, command in the name of the capitalist. The work of supervision becomes their established and exclusive function.
>
> op. cit.

1.4.3 Chapter 14. Division of Labour and Manufacture

Having reflected on the kind of world which capitalism has created through the combination of their military-like command of the mass of the population with their unceasing revolutionizing of the labour process, Marx continues here to reflect on the nature of modern manufacturing, now sharply different from the relics of the old handicraft type of manufacture from which it emerged.

1.4.4 Chapter 15. Machinery and Modern Industry

Marx uses an historical review of the development of manufacture through various phases from the middle of the 16th century up to his own time to trace the evolution of modern industrial manufacture. This essay is not relevant to the Hegelian roots of Marx's method so I will leave it be.

1.5 *Part v. The Production of Absolute and of Relative Surplus-Value*

1.5.1 Chapter 16. Absolute and Relative Surplus Value

Here Marx reflects on the notion of *productive labour*. In Marx's day, prior to Frederick Taylor (1911), capitalists regarded as a "productive" worker only those who were "hands-on" operatives, and sought to reduce the number of supervisory staff.

But once labour has become social labour and not merely the labour of individuals, thanks to the division of labour, "In order to labour productively, it is no longer necessary for you to do manual work yourself; enough, if you are an organ of the collective labourer, and perform one of its subordinate functions." Labour is not to be framed in the terms of individual labour; in the modern division of labour terms such as necessary and surplus labour time no longer make sense in relation to each worker taken individually. However, they remain true of the "collective labourer."

> On the other hand, however, our notion of productive labour becomes narrowed. Capitalist production is not merely the production of commodities, it is essentially the production of surplus-value. The labourer produces, not for himself, but for capital. It no longer suffices, therefore, that he should simply produce. He must produce surplus-value. That labourer alone is productive, who produces surplus-value for the capitalist, and thus works for the self-expansion of capital.
>
> MARX, 1867, Chapter 16

Noteworthy here, albeit incidentally, is Marx's reference to the labour of a school teacher:

> If we may take an example from outside the sphere of production of material objects, a schoolmaster is a productive labourer when, in addition to belabouring the heads of his scholars, he works like a horse to enrich the school proprietor. That the latter has laid out his capital in a teaching factory, instead of in a sausage factory, does not alter the relation.
>
> op. cit.

What is important is labour as a "social relation of production, a relation that has sprung up historically and stamps the labourer as the direct means of creating surplus-value. To be a *productive labourer* is, therefore, not a piece of luck, but a misfortune."

Marx emphasises the transformative impact of industrial capitalism on social life:

> The production of absolute surplus-value turns exclusively upon the length of the working-day; the production of relative surplus-value, revolutionises out and out the technical processes of labour, and the

> composition of society. It therefore presupposes a specific mode, the capitalist mode of production, a mode which, along with its methods, means, and conditions, arises and develops itself spontaneously on the foundation afforded by the formal subjection of labour to capital. In the course of this development, the formal subjection is replaced by the real subjection of labour to capital.
>
> op. cit.

The new unit introduced in this part is the productive worker who is no longer taken to be simply a wage-worker, but a wage-worker insofar as they employed in the production of value as part of the "collective labourer."

Marx uses the remainder of this part to provide an overview of the transformation of human life wrought by industrial capitalism by means of its revolution in technology, its expansion of the working day to the limits of human endurance and the continued impoverishment of an increasing mass of the population.

1.6 *Part VI. Wages*

The subject matter of Part VI is wages – value of a day's labour-power. Payment by the day in money is the universal form of wage and constitutes the *unit* in this division. Other forms of payment for the hire of labour-power, such as payment in kind, piece work and payment by the hour, are *derivative forms* of wage, and their use makes no fundamental change in the nature of wages as payment for labour-time, but are merely methods of disciplining the workforce. Likewise, work conducted under a contract covering more extended periods of working time is to be taken as another particular form of work, in this case modified somewhat to the benefit of the worker.

1.6.1 The Remaining Parts of Volume One of *Capital*

Part VII is on the accumulation of capital, moving from simple reproduction, through the accumulation of surplus value to formulate the "General Law of Capitalist Development."

> The greater the social wealth, the functioning capital, the extent and energy of its growth, and, therefore, also the absolute mass of the proletariat and the productiveness of its labour, the greater is the industrial reserve army. The same causes which develop the expansive power of capital, develop also the labour power at its disposal. The relative mass of the industrial reserve army increases therefore with the potential energy of wealth. But the greater this reserve army in proportion to the active

> labour army, the greater is the mass of a consolidated surplus population, whose misery is in inverse ratio to its torment of labour. The more extensive, finally, the lazarus layers of the working class, and the industrial reserve army, the greater is official pauperism. *This is the absolute general law of capitalist accumulation.* Like all other laws it is modified in its working by many circumstances, the analysis of which does not concern us here.
>
> MARX, 1867, Chapter 25

Here Marx reviews the historical development of capitalism, highlighting how capitalist development has revolutionised daily life, the class structure of the country and the labour process itself. Everywhere its impact has been both modernizing and devastating to the lives of the masses.

Part VIII is again an historical review, this time covering primitive accumulation, the sheer robbery by which the initial masses of money were gathered in the hands of a few individuals and the impoverished mass of unemployed labourers whose labour could be exploited concentrated in the towns.

> In the history of primitive accumulation, all revolutions are epoch-making that act as levers for the capital class in course of formation; but, above all, those moments when great masses of men are suddenly and forcibly torn from their means of subsistence, and hurled as free and "unattached" proletarians on the labour-market. The expropriation of the agricultural producer, of the peasant, from the soil, is the basis of the whole process. The history of this expropriation, in different countries, assumes different aspects, and runs through its various phases in different orders of succession, and at different periods. In England alone, which we take as our example, has it the classic form.
>
> MARX, 1867, Chapter 26

The point is that the methods of primitive accumulation created the conditions for modern industrial capitalism, but did away with the conditions for their own method of enrichment. By its nature, outright robbery only works once. Industrial capital continuously reproduces the conditions for its own existence, and this is one of the problems which must be addressed in Volume Two of *Capital.*

This part also deals with the activity of the capitalists in Parliament and in colonisation. The most significant attribute of industrial capitalism is the concentration of social wealth in the hands of ever fewer capitalists.

> Centralisation of the means of production and socialisation of labour at last reach a point where they become incompatible with their capitalist integument. This integument is burst asunder. The knell of capitalist private property sounds. The expropriators are expropriated.
>
> MARX, 1867, Chapter 32

At the turn of the century, Kautsky (1892), leader of the German Socialists, believed that the concentration of capital in ever fewer hands alongside the immiseration of the masses guaranteed the victory of Socialism. Alas! this process did not culminate in the final crisis of capitalism.

The concentration of capital, Marx believes, is one of those secular historical processes which must at some point lead to an historical crisis of capitalism. This theme can only be fully developed on the basis of developments which still lie ahead of us in Volume Three, however.

Interesting as all this is, being a product of Marx's lifetime study of capitalist development, in the first six parts the development of the principles in Volume One of *Capital* have been completed. I will now review what has been achieved by *Capital* Volume One with respect to Marx's conceptual reconstruction of capitalism as a whole by using Hegel's method outlined in the *Logic*.

1.7 Capital *Volume One, Conclusion*

Marx has revealed the fundamental laws of development of bourgeois society by the application of Hegel's method as set out in the passage of the *Logic* entitled "The Idea of the True," and based on a study of the history of bourgeois development and a critique of the contemporary science of value, Political Economy.

The germ cell which marked the starting point for political economy was the simplest social form of value, the *commodity*. Simple commodity production was an analytical abstraction corresponding to the earliest development of the bourgeoisie in the guilds and companies of the middle ages – *bourgeois society*. The crucial outcome of this phase of development was the circulation of commodities, and of *money* as a universal commodity, and the development of the forces of production and social conditions to a point where *capitalist* development had become possible.

Volume One does not follow the development of money beyond gold. That gold has long since proved inadequate for most of the demands of post-modern capitalism for a means of payment, etc., simply means that it will be necessary to take Marx's analysis *further*, and does not invalidate Marx's analysis as far as it went. Likewise, *Capital* was written on the assumption of a national economy sharing the same currency, and imported materials were what you could call "boundary objects."

On this topic, it should also be mentioned that Marx does not analyse the use-value of a commodity, even though he subjected its exchange value to analysis extensively. The commodity is thus taken to be the typical industrial product: tons of steel, yards of cloth and numbers of shoes. In Chapter 16 he says: "a schoolmaster is a productive labourer when, in addition to belabouring the heads of his scholars, he works like a horse to enrich the school proprietor," thus making it clear that a commodity can be a service, so long as it is made for exchange. In his times, schools were generally run by churches, and the "service industry" was largely oriented to the personal consumption of surplus value by the wealthy. Intellectual property was a reality in Marx's day, too, but Marx makes no mention of this type of commodity. But if you were going to extend *Capital* to today's condition, an analysis of use-value is needed. In such a study, the industrial product would constitute the universal commodity.

The germ cell which marked the starting point of a new division of the subject matter in Part II was a new form of value, *capital*, beginning from a germ cell in the form of Mr. Moneybags, the embryonic capitalist firm and unit of capital. Moneybags bought commodities in order to sell more dearly: M–C–M'. Moneybags' appearance corresponded to the transformation of the mediaeval guild master into an industrial capitalist, alongside the merchant capitalist and the usurer.

It may seem that the employment of wage-labour is not the sole or even best way of amassing capital. However, once we make a distinction between capitalists *sharing surplus value amongst themselves* and *extracting* surplus value in the first place, Marx will be seen to be correct.

The germ cell which marked the starting point for Part III was *unpaid labour-time*, a new form of value, surplus-value. Unpaid labour arises only in the conditions of the exploitation of labour-power in the process of capital accumulation. Industrial capital is the universal form of capital, surpassing usurious and commercial capital, which nonetheless continued to exist alongside it.

Looked at from the present day, with all our computers, apps. and automatons, this may sound like an anachronism. Don't fool yourself. The widely recognised mental health crisis is testimony to the appetite capitalism has for our vital energies, and they are measured fundamentally by time.

The germ cell which marked the starting point for Part IV was *necessary labour time*. Analysis of the necessary labour time shows that the revolutionising of the forces of production wrought by industrial capital leads to a gradual reduction in the number of hours of average labour required to produce the equivalent of the necessities of life for the labourer of the time.

The unit for Part VI is the daily wage, paid in money sufficient for the worker to renew their labour ready to work the next day and the next generation. Other forms of payment for labour-power, such as piece work, are particular forms of wage.

The unit for Part VII is the *productive worker* whose labour is a share in the "collective worker" which is the producer of surplus value in modern capitalist industry. Not every wage worker is a productive worker, the wages of servants for example are paid for out of accumulated surplus value.

With these units, Marx has constructed the first "layer" in the conceptual reconstruction of industrial capitalism. In this layer of the theory, commodities are exchanged at their value, capital is accumulated by the direct expropriation of value by means of unpaid labour, paid for by the day in money. The resulting process leads to an increasing mass of impoverished labourers being drawn into the process of production of surplus value, the extension of the working day to its limits to the neglect of the conditions of a genuinely human life, and the concentration of social wealth in the hands of a few wealthy capitalists.

•••

Forgive me dear reader if I could suggest that even if you are reading Marx or any kind of economic text for the first time this line of argument is abundantly clear. Granted, comparing it to the facts of present-day or historical capitalism is another matter. Indeed, Marx himself has already pointed out that the development of Volume One stands in flagrant contradiction to the well-known empirical fact that the rate of profit on capital is not proportional to the portion of that capital taken by wages. Perhaps you are doubtful, but the line of argument is clear, is it not?

And yet, not only have you read and understood Marx's epoch-making work, but you have also seen how it was composed according to the method of Hegel's *Logic*.

I will just make a couple of points.

First of all, the method of deduction applied by Marx is not the formal syllogistic type of logic taught in school. The first and chief difficulty in using this type of logic is *selecting* the right datum from which to begin the analysis. Hegel characterised as the "germ cell" the prius which makes the starting point at each stage of the conceptual reconstruction. In 1867, everyone knew about the commodity, and by 1821 Ricardo had established commodities as the starting point for analysis! Nevertheless, in general, *selecting* this datum is somewhat a matter of art, so to speak. In this case Marx had the benefit of an established, if problematic, science. Further, Hegel demanded that having selected the prius, the researcher must resist the temptation to throw on to the table "other factors," but instead retain the focus strictly to the analysis of the unit, disclosing what is *within* the unit. Marx was the first to bring this discipline, learnt from Hegel's *Logic*, to economic science.

The researcher must analyse this datum, and here again what to do is somewhat of an art; the researcher must identify a *contradiction* within the subject matter. And not just any contradiction, but one which takes the researcher one more step towards understanding and "reconstructing" the whole phenomenon. Analysis of the germ cell uncovers other empirically given features of the phenomenon now shown to be necessary features beginning from the germ cell. This analysis prepares the way for synthesis of additional features of the phenomenon at a later stage in the synthesis.

In the first chapter, I discussed how Hegel advised the researcher how to select the unit and reveal its internal contradiction. In the *Logic* and the *Encyclopaedia* as a whole, Hegel gave us literally hundreds of examples of how to do this. Every subject matter has a different content and every science built on this content is unique. But just as we practice our scales before we try to play Beethoven on the piano, so we can study Hegel's *Logic* to become fluent in this kind of logic. There is no formula for this.

So the whole line of argument in Volume One of *Capital* is "Hegelian," supplemented in the latter part of the work with reflections on the historical development of capitalism.

Secondly, Marx has already drawn attention to the fact that the uniform rate of surplus value, derived from the analysis of value as abstract labour-time, is in contradiction to the empirical fact that the rate of profit on capital which is generally uniform across an economy. So what are we left with at the end of Volume One, especially given that Volumes Two and Three would not be published by Engels till 12 years after Marx's death?

It is in the nature of the "rate of surplus value" that it is a characteristic not of an individual capitalist firm but of an *entire economy* – with its natural resources, its human material and customs and habits. The rate of surplus value is not calculated on the basis of any capitalist's wage bill or the total value of any capitalist's product. It depends on the *socially average labour embodied in the customary subsistence life of an average worker in the community*. Part IV on relative surplus value would not make sense otherwise.

We are accustomed however to associating the "rate of profit on capital" with an *individual* unit of capital, an individual firm. This irrespective of the fact that the profit of each capitalist will approximate a general rate of profit which tends to be uniform across the economy, across different industries, with different average proportions of living labour in the production process of each sector of the economy.

The relation between the rate of profit and the socially determined rate of surplus value depends on the "organic composition of capital," the proportion of constant capital in the total investment of capital. This is a contradiction which Marx has told us will not be resolved until later, and in the meantime the calculation of the rate of profit for each individual capital, as given in Volume One, will not be correct if applied to capitalist firms as they are actually found! If every unit of capital had the same proportion of capital invested in constant capital there would there be a uniform ratio between the rate of profit and the rate of surplus value. But this of course not the case.

However! All of Marx's calculations are based on *averages*, that is to say, *totals* taken across the whole economy, divided by the number of … workers, capitals, products, or whatever. The logic is watertight insofar as it refers to the *total* mass of surplus value, the total necessary labour and total means of production across the whole economy. Marx has computed *exactly* the mass of surplus value appropriated by the capitalist class every year which can then be shared amongst themselves, and *exactly* the amount of social labour which has been devoted to the subsistence of the working population, and *exactly* the annual value of the means of production consumed in production. I am indebted to Fred Moseley (2016) for this decisive observation.

That is, Marx has analysed the *universal* capital, having begun from the germ cell formed when Moneybags began to exploit labour-power by forcing his employees to work for unpaid labour-time – the universal form of capital.

> The progress, proper to the Notion, from universal to particular, is the basis and the possibility of a *synthetic science*, of a *system* and of *systematic cognition*. (Hegel, 1816, §1733)

This is no small accomplishment, but all that has been determined is the distribution of value in one cycle of production. That still leaves the problem of reproducing the conditions for the next cycle. If the capitalists simply consumed the product for their own enjoyment that would be the end of capitalism.

One final comment. The historical thread guiding this analysis is surely unmistakeable? The history I am referring to is not that of the succession of different dominant modes of production throughout history, but the historical development of *each of the specific relations* which have reached their zenith in modern capitalism. The result is narratives which are both logical and historical at the same time, "categorical genealogies."

So two problems remain outstanding: (1) how *the various classes and their means of production are reproduced* year after year and (2) how the various classes *divide their share of the product amongst themselves*. Only then will the great contradiction between the rate of surplus value and the rate of profit be resolved.

The solution of each of these problems will prove again to involve specific new ethical regimes.

2 Marx's *Capital* Volume Two: the Process of Circulation of Capital

In Volume One, Marx laid the foundations for a conceptual reconstruction of capital, but the results were still at odds with empirical reality in some respects and some questions left unanswered.

Specifically, Marx had derived the *total value* produced by an individual unit of capital in each cycle of production and its distribution between the working class, the capitalist class, and that portion necessarily reinvested by all units of capital in means of production. But he had not shown how capital reproduced itself cycle after cycle, not just in terms of value, but in terms of the material products required for the continuation of social life and the reproduction of capital.

Secondly, although he had demonstrated how the use of wage labour allowed the industrial capitalist to extract surplus value from the workers, he had not addressed how this surplus value was distributed among the capitalist class as a whole because each capital was treated on its own independently of any interaction with other capitals. This task, as it happens, means solving the riddle of the contradiction between the rate of profit and the rate of surplus value.

Volume One considered each unit of capital operating side by side with other units of capital, all exchanging their products at their value. But no consideration had been given as to how the social conditions and the materials needed for production were to be continuously made available for use by a capital. Each unit of capital, after all, executed only one of the innumerable functions needed for continuation of social life. How were all these separate units of capital to renew themselves for each cycle of production?

Marx had died in 1883, two years before the publication of Volume Two, and it was left to Engels to assemble the notes and drafts left by Marx. Engels explained in the Preface the enormously complex task Marx had bequeathed him. However, I defer to the opinion of most scholars who have studied these manuscripts in detail and their opinion that Engels provided us a text which will for the most part "represent exclusively the work of its author, not of its editor."

2.1 *Part I. The Metamorphoses of Capital and Their Circuits*

2.1.1 Chapter 1. The Circuit of Money Capital

The circuit of industrial capital is the object of Part I of Volume Two, and Marx begins with the *universal form of the circuit of industrial capital*, in which money-capital is transformed into productive capital which in turn transforms itself into commodity-capital, which is transformed back into money-capital, but now at an expanded level.

Marx expands the circuit introduced in Volume One, M–C–M', to include production. Thus: M–C ... P ... C'–M', in which P represents the process of production of the product, the transformation of commodities, C, into a new commodity, C'. In Volume One, "the various forms which capital takes on in its different stages ... were not considered. These forms are now the direct object of our study."

Even though each circuit will in fact be realised by many different units of capital, it is not the interaction between units of capital which is the object here. Rather, the capitals here act as links in the chains which connect the outputs from a capital around to it inputs through a multiplicity of metamorphoses. The conception resembles that of food chains in an ecosystem.

Consistent with Hegel's requirement that the new unit be considered in its own right:

> In order to conceive these forms in their pure state, one must first of all discard all factors which have nothing to do with the changing or building of the forms as such. It is therefore taken for granted here not only that the commodities are sold at their values but also that this takes place under the same conditions throughout. Likewise disregarded therefore are any changes of value which might occur during the movement in circuits.
>
> MARX, 1885, Chapter 1

In the course of this chapter, Marx examines each phase of the circuit, and reflects on the multiple obstacles the circuit has to navigate for the process of industrial capital to reproduce itself. Workers must be paid at short, regular intervals if they are to live and there must be an adequate supply of their needs on the market when they are paid; labour and means of production circulate in two entirely different markets and both markets must be able to supply the needs of production continuously as required by the production schedule. If an excess of product is produced it cannot be converted into money, but if not enough product is produced, then the cycle will be interrupted at some other point. Marx notes that these conditions presuppose a high degree of development of the circulation of commodities.

Thus Marx introduces the unit of reproduction (or life-process) of industrial capital, the metamorphosis, or "circuit" of capital, in its universal form.

> Industrial capital is the only mode of existence of capital in which not only the appropriation of surplus-value, or surplus-product, but simultaneously its creation is a *function* of capital. Therefore with it the capitalist character of production is a necessity. Its existence implies the class antagonism between capitalists and wage-labourers. To the extent that it seizes control of social production, the technique and social organisation of the labour-process are revolutionised and with them the economico-historical type of society.
>
> op. cit.

In less developed forms of capital, the workers may go back to the village when manufacturing work is slack, products it does not produce itself may be supplied by merchants, and so on. In industrial capitalism, however, *all* the products it needs must be made available by itself, by industrial capital.

Marx also contrasts this circuit to other forms of capital, such as in the transport industry, where it is the productive process itself which is the useful product. Although, like all capital it begins and ends with money. The same observation would apply to all the service industries.

After reprising much of what had already been established in Volume One, Marx says:

> What lies behind $M{-}C<^{L}_{MP}$ [Labour & Means of Production] is distribution; not distribution in the ordinary meaning of a distribution of articles of consumption, but the distribution of the elements of production itself, the material factors of which are concentrated on one side, and labour-power, isolated, on the other. ... capitalist production, once it is established, not only reproduces this separation but extends its scope further and further until it becomes the prevailing condition.
>
> op. cit.

Capitalist production reproduces to an ever-increasing extent the class of wage-labourers, and therefore pre-supposes a sufficient mass of productive capital. In the second stage of the circuit, productive capital, "the capital-value has acquired a bodily form in which it cannot continue to circulate but must enter into consumption, viz., into productive consumption."

In order to live, the workers must be employed repeatedly at short intervals and always find sufficient means of subsistence available on the market, having long since been separated from petty agriculture which formerly supported the labourer in troubled times. These conditions presuppose a high degree of development of the circulation of commodities. Likewise, each unit of productive capital requires for its functioning the uninterrupted availability of means of production, the products of other units of productive capital.

After presenting the *universal* form of the circuit of capital in industrial capitalism, beginning as in every stage of capitalism, with a sum of money, Marx presents the *particular* forms of circulation: the circuit of production-capital (embodied in the living labour of employees and the means of production) and the circuit of commodity-capital.

Marx also briefly examines the credit economy which arises on the basis of circulation and supply-and-demand. He will then examine the time and cost of circulation in general, and move to look at particular costs of circulation (retail and wholesale selling and buying, storage and transportation).

Thus the *unit* in Part I is *the circuit of capital* through its different value-forms, and developed from universal to particular. These observations are sufficient to confirm that in Volume Two, whose subject matter is the *reproduction of a capitalist social formation*, Marx is continuing with the Hegelian method adopted in Volume One.

The circuit which begins and ends with money is the universal form; interlaced with the universal form are the particular forms: the circuit (reproduction) of production-capital and the circuit of commodity capital.

2.1.2 Chapter 2. The Circuit of Productive Capital

> The circuit of productive capital has the general formula P ... C'–M'–C ... P. It signifies the periodical renewal of the functioning of productive capital, hence its reproduction.
>
> MARX, 1885, Chapter 2

Marx here examines the metamorphosis of capital in industrial capitalism, this time beginning not with a sum of money-capital, but with productive capital. From this point of view circulation proper appears as an instrument promoting the periodically renewed reproduction of the productive process, rendered continuous by its renewal.

This circuit is firstly I. Simple Reproduction and then II. Accumulation and Reproduction on an Extended Scale.

In the *simple reproduction* of productive capital, assuming that, as in the first chapter, conditions remain constant and that commodities are bought and sold at their values, the entire surplus-value enters into the personal consumption of the capitalist, the surplus value being spent either for commodities proper or for personal services to himself or family. The *general form* is reproduction on an extended scale, with the investment of surplus value into further production of surplus value.

2.1.3 Chapter 3. The Circuit of Commodity-Capital

The Circuit of Commodity-Capital is represented as C'–M'–C ... P ... C'.

However,

> it is no longer sufficient to confine oneself to indicating that the metamorphoses C'–M' and M–C are on the one hand functionally defined sections in the metamorphoses of capital, on the other are links in the general circulation of commodities. It becomes necessary to elucidate the intertwining of the metamorphoses of one individual capital with those of other individual capitals and with that part of the total product which is intended for individual consumption. On analysing the circuit of an individual industrial capital, we therefore base our studies mainly on the first two forms.
>
> MARX, 1885, Chapter 3

Marx has said that the object being examined in Part I is the circulation of capital, and he has analysed the *universal* form which begins and ends with money. He has thus analysed circulation into three phases and brought out the problems which arise in each phase. The real subject matter here is only named in Part III, the *reproduction* of the aggregate social capital in all its constituent forms.

In the same sense that capital rests on the commodity, reproduction of capital at the broadest level rests on the circuit of capital by a series of metamorphoses through the various value-forms beginning with money and ending with money. The circuit of a single unit of capital is the unit of analysis for the reproduction of capitalist society.

In the remaining chapters of Part I, Marx studies a number of issues arising from circulation of capital through the commodity market and production.

Chapter 4, "The Three Formulas of the Circuit" shows that in all forms of the circulation of capital "The self-expansion of value as the determining purpose, as the compelling motive." However, every point in the circuit depends on the completion of the whole circuit for its own reproduction. Every social function then is dependent on the continuity of capital accumulation. Each of these functions then cannot be understood in itself, but only in its arising from and returning to the circulation of capital. In the process, the social fabric is continuously transformed into an image of capital in its successive forms.

Chapter 5, "The Time of Circulation" shows that in addition to the production time already dealt with in the calculation of the rates of profit and surplus value, capital also spends time in circulation in the commodity form before returning to production in the form of labour and means of production. The time required for reproduction of capital is in excess of the labour-time. But circulation time outside of production "creates neither value nor surplus-value." The circulation time required for the reproduction of the factors of production is "a condition of the process of production."

The time spent in realising surplus value is therefore necessarily *paid for out of the surplus value* appropriated during production, but it neither increases nor decreases the mass of surplus value.

Likewise Chapter 6, "The costs of circulation" and Chapter 7 "The costs of storage and transportation" show that these necessary expenses are *deductions* from the surplus value created during the production process.

> The general law is that all costs of circulation, which arise only from changes in the forms of commodities do not add to their value.
>
> MARX, 1885, Chapter 6

2.1.4 Summary of Part I

Approaching the problem of the reproduction of capital as an entire social formation, Marx takes the simplest social form of the reproduction of capitalist social relations to be the *circulation of capital* through a series metamorphoses beginning with money. Each phase of this circuit is essential to the reproduction of capital and the myriad of social functions which are necessary to its reproduction. This conception is somewhat analogous to the "food web" known to ecologists.

His analysis showed that this process is carried as a cost to surplus value and paid for out of the proceeds of capital gained through the appropriation of unpaid labour-time.

2.2 *Part II. The Turnover of Capital*

2.2.1 Chapter 7. The Turnover Time and Number of Turnovers

In Part II the object is *turnover* – the time lapse between when capital is advanced until it returns ready for a new cycle of expansion. The issue here is specifically the multiplying effect that reduction of the circulation time of capital has on the annual rate of profit. The problem of turnover arises as the quantitative measure of the process analysed in Part I.

> We have seen that the entire time of turnover of a given capital is equal to the sum of its time of circulation and its time of production. It is the period of time from the moment of the advance of capital-value in a definite form to the return of the functioning capital-value in the same form. The compelling motive of capitalist production is always the creation of surplus-value by means of the advanced value, no matter whether this value is advanced in its independent form, i.e., in the money-form, or in commodities.
>
> MARX, 1885, Chapter 7

The turnover time of capital is the time taken for capital to complete the circuit and return, in expanded quantity to the form in which it started, be that commodities or money.

> From the point of view of the capitalist, the time of turnover of his capital is the time for which he must advance his capital in order to create surplus-value with it and receive it back in its original shape.
>
> op. cit.

2.2.2 Chapter 8. Fixed Capital and Circulating Capital

Beginning from this general form, Marx differentiates the process of the turnover into two forms: fixed and circulating capital. Fixed and circulating capital are categories already well-known to political economy, unlike constant and variable capital which are original innovations by Marx.

This method, which we see time and again, in which Marx identifies a unit in its general form and then *analyses* into parts, moving from universal to particular, is in line with the method proposed by Hegel in "The Idea of the True."

It turns out that although "fixed" capital does not generally circulate as such, it is consumed and subject to turnover time, variable according to the type of fixed capital.

Fixed capital (the instruments of labour) and "fluid" capital (fuel, oil and such like as well as maintenance and repairs, together with the raw material incorporated in the product) must be renewed, over variable periods of time. The overall time required for this component of capital advanced must be determined as an average over these very diverse periods of reproduction.

The labour-power incorporated into the product must be renewed by the worker through purchase and consumption of their means of subsistence, and is thus part of circulating capital. Capital must be advanced for "fluid" capital and labour-power only for the period during the period during which production is underway. Fixed capital is renewed over a longer period of time according to the durability of the various components of the means of production.

The costs of maintaining capital sunk into fixed capital appears to the capitalist like an unproductive hoard. A credit system would allow this capital to function as productive capital through the interest paid on such capital borrowed for the purpose of purchasing and maintaining fixed capital.

The following chapters criticise the theories of the Political Economists on the question of turnover and investigates the various problems which arise here.

The principle outcome is the impact of the turnover time of capital on the "Annual Rate of Surplus Value" in Chapter 16, where Marx says that:

> The capital employed in the production of the annual quantity of surplus-value is equal to the advanced capital multiplied by the number of its turnovers, which we shall call *n*.

and

> The annual rate of surplus-value is equal to the (real rate of surplus-value × variable capital advanced × *n*) / (variable capital advanced)
>
> MARX, 1885, Chapter 16

This makes it clear that alongside the requirement of capital to reproduce the social conditions for its own reproduction, the motive force of capital, the *annual* rate of surplus value, drives it to turn over its capital invested in fixed capital as quickly as possible.

2.3 *Part III. The Reproduction and Circulation of Aggregate Social Capital*

In the form of an Introduction to Part III, Marx presents his own summary of "the story so far" which is interesting in itself. Marx now links the circulation of capital examined already in Volume Two with the segmentation of capital into constant, variable and surplus capital in Volume One.

Reflecting on the circulation of capital as both money and commodities, he notes that this capital consists of only two components:

> 1) The circuit of capital proper and 2) the circuit of the commodities which enter into individual consumption, consequently of the commodities for which the labourer expends his wages and the capitalist his surplus-value (or a part of it). At any rate, the circuit of capital comprises also the circulation of the surplus-value, since the latter is a part of the commodity capital, and likewise the conversion of the variable capital into labour-power, the payment of wages.
>
> MARX, 1885, Chapter 18

The circulation of surplus value entails the production of commodities which do not form a link in the circulation of capital, in particular commodities for personal consumption (rather than commodities for use in production such as raw materials, machinery, etc.), and the expenditure of the surplus value for the personal enjoyment of the capitalist. But this surplus value also includes a myriad of activities outside the circle of reproduction of capital such as the maintenance of the state apparatus.

All the individual capitals which are reproducing themselves as described in earlier chapters are locked together in interlacing circuits, and Marx observes:

> But in both the first and the second Volumes it was always only a question of some individual capital, of the movement of some individualised part of social capital. ... We have now to study the process of circulation (which in its entirety is a form of the process of reproduction) of the individual capitals as components of the aggregate social capital, that is to say, the process of circulation of this aggregate social capital.
>
> op. cit.

Money-capital and its reproduction and expansion is the prime mover of the entire aggregate social capital. The magnitude of the money which must be advanced is continuously increased due to the withdrawal of money from circulation in the production process which is demanding ever-larger investment in constant capital. As a result, the demand for credit, which Marx has not yet considered, sharpens.

The object which Marx is now addressing is the reproduction of each of the parts of capital identified in the first volume: constant capital, variable capital and surplus value. From analysing the reproduction of capital as a whole, universally, he now moves to the particular in this sense, the reproduction of each of its parts: the constant, variable and surplus capital. Each particular segment of value of production is reproduced by its own circuit, beginning with money, its transformation into a certain kind of product in the form of commodities, and its return to the form of money-capital.

In the course of these circuits, the commodities in each segment of the social body are consumed, respectively in the production of means of production (Department One), the production of labour-power in working class households and the production of luxury goods and services for the benefit of the capitalist class (Department Two).

After Chapter 19 which is devoted to polemics with the Political Economists, Marx discusses these two Departments in an extensive Chapter 20.

Each of the two departments which must produce commodities to more or less match the demand for the reproduction of constant, variable and surplus value, each demand a proportion of constant, variable and surplus capital. Marx endeavours to trace the complex demands for the reproduction of the entire social capital through the interlacing of these distinct circuits of reproduction.

The production of constant, variable and surplus capital in a single cycle of reproduction and expansion of capital by individual units of capital, and every such unit can only go on so long as money is put into circulation and withdrawn, while at the same time each of the components of the production process, are realised not only in their value, but in their material substance. In this way capitalist appropriation reproduces itself at the same time as reproducing the social and material conditions for the existence of the entire social formation of capitalism.

Chapters 20 and 21 are exceedingly long. Hegel's approach, again illustrated with Marx's approach to analysis of the reproduction of capital, has now led Marx to a consideration of particulars which no longer hold any interest from the point of view of tracing the influence of Hegel on *Capital*, the subject of this book. I will offer no further analysis of the subject matters of these two chapters.

2.4 *Summary of Volume Two*

The subject matter of Volume Two is the reproduction of the entire social formation in which the capitalist mode of accumulation and production exists.

Volume Two complements Volume One which demonstrated how labour takes the form of value as "abstract labour-time," and the total value was divided into three component parts: constant capital which exists in the form of material products used in production of commodities, variable capital which accrues to the working class for their subsistence, and surplus value accruing to the capitalist class.

To do this, Marx treated capital as if it were one single social capital operating in the form of individual units of capital. Volume One had not shown where these components of capital came from and where they went, or how these individual units could work together to sustain and reproduce the entire social organism.

Marx needed to demonstrate how this cycle of exploitation was reproduced in an entire social formation. This was to be the business of Volume Two.

The subject matter is the production and reproduction of the entire social formation of industrial capitalism. The unit of analysis is the circuit of money-capital through productive-capital and commodity-capital and back in expanded form to money. This unit is simply the further analysis of the same unit identified in Part II of Volume One, "The Transformation of Money into Capital," the commodity relation mediated by money: M–C–M' to include production which transforms the inputs to production, C, into the product, C', i.e., C–P ... C'–M'.

Part III of Volume Two has shown that

> the capitalist process of production taken as a whole represents *a synthesis of the processes of production and circulation.*
>
> MARX, 1894

When we are led to contemplate how interlaced are all the processes abstracted from the social production process we can appreciate the power of Marx's original abstraction. His initial object was the division of the social product between the working class and the capitalist class. To discover this he had to analyse the single unit, commodity exchange, moving then to the use of money as a means of payment C–M–C' and from there to the single unit of capital, M–C–M'. Systematically, Marx has synthesised the reproductive process of the entire social formation. A wage of a factory worker contains a component arising from the cost of bread which in turn depends on the cost of maintaining a baker's oven which in turn depends on the supply of bricks, etc., etc., etc.

Everything so far as been based on the assumption of commodities being sold at their value and has assumed that the value of products remains stable throughout each circuit.

Marx has already identified a problem which manifests itself in the first two volumes based on the circulation of commodities exchanged at their values. This assumption, which is real and verifiable so long as independent producers exchange their own products, has been extended to circumstances where the products being circulated are the *products of industrial capital* and no worker can identify any commodity as being the product of his or her own labour. Workers are employed in complex processes of production in which each product passes through the hands of many workers and absorbs the value of machinery and raw material, likewise the products of industrial capital.

The ethos of the equality of all human labour underlies the distribution of the total social labour, the value of all commodities and is reflected in the purchase and sale of labour-power.

Industrial capitalism is a society in which units of capital exchange products and a new ethos is in place. The outstanding problem which Marx must now face is the resolution of this contradiction, manifested in the co-existence of a single rate of surplus value characteristic of a single national economy, and a general rate of profit enjoyed by all units of capital alike.

Nor has Marx yet addressed how the surplus value is shared by the industrial capitalist (who has come into possession of it by the exploitation of labour-power and the use of means of production) with the banker who advanced the money-capital with which the cycle of reproduction began, and the landlord whose charges for rent appear in the industrial capitalists' account books as *costs* alongside interest. In fact, the circulation of capital in the financial market has so far lain outside the scope of Marx's analysis.

These are the subject matters of Volume Three which completes the conceptual reconstruction of the capitalist mode of production.

3 Marx's *Capital* Volume Three: the Process of Capitalist Production as a Whole

As is made clear in Engels' Preface, Volume Three is addressed first and above all to the resolution of the contradiction between the law of value, established in Volume One, suggesting a universal rate of surplus value along with the empirically given fact of a uniform rate of profit across different sectors of the economy, irrespective of the composition of capital. At the time of publication of Volume Three, 11 years after Marx's death, Engels was able to review a plethora of proposed solutions to this contradiction among the Political Economists. Accordingly, Part I is entitled "The Conversion of Surplus-Value into Profit and of the Rate of Surplus-Value into the Rate of Profit."

Here Marx is following Hegel's advice:

> Analytic cognition ... starts from ... a problem, that is to say, given only in its circumstances and conditions, but not yet disengaged from them and presented on its own account in simple self-subsistence.
>
> HEGEL, 1816

At the same time as resolving this fundamental problem in political economy, Marx introduces the process of *distribution* of the total surplus value between different units of capital across the economy. Volume Three presents *a synthesis* of the processes of production presented in Volume One, and the circulation of capital, presented in Volume Two.

The basic units are the same as those introduced in Volume One, but Marx moves from the universal individual unit of capital to particular units of capital representing different sectors of industrial capitalism, alongside units of finance capital and rent-seeking capital. Further, the individual units of capital are now taken as *parts* of the social whole of capital, rather than independent units, each with its own cycle of reproduction.

This synthesis will provide for the first time a conceptual reconstruction of the capitalist social formation *as a whole*.

3.1 *Part I. The Conversion of Surplus-Value into Profit and of the Rate of Surplus-Value into the Rate of Profit*

Marx's opening words summing up the narrative which has brought us to this stage of his account are worth quoting verbatim.

> In Volume One we analysed the phenomena which constitute the *process of capitalist production* as such, as the immediate productive process, with no regard for any of the secondary effects of outside influences. But this immediate process of production does not exhaust the life span of capital. It is supplemented in the actual world by the *process of circulation*, which was the object of study in Volume Two. In the latter, namely in Part III, which treated the process of circulation as a medium for the process of social reproduction, it developed that the capitalist process of production taken as a whole represents *a synthesis of the processes of production and circulation*.
>
> Considering what this third book treats, it cannot confine itself to general reflection relative to this synthesis. On the contrary, it must locate and describe the concrete forms which grow out of the *movements of capital as a whole*.

> In their actual movement, capitals confront each other in such concrete shape, for which the form of capital in the immediate process of production, just as its form in the process of circulation, appear only as special instances. The various forms of capital, as evolved in this book, thus approach step by step the form which they assume on the surface of society, in the action of different capitals upon one another, in competition, and in the ordinary consciousness of the agents of production themselves.
>
> MARX, 1894, Chapter 1

Thus Marx introduces Volume Three as the final phase of the conceptual reconstruction of capitalism, synthesising the direct accumulation of surplus value, its circulation across the entire social formation, and the distribution of surplus between different sections of the capitalist class. This includes first the different sectors of productive capital, and then finance capital and landed capital. The synthesis now approaches the forms capital assumes on the surface of society and in the everyday consciousness of the denizens of capitalist society with their ordinary common sense.

The object which is the subject matter of analysis is the "movements of capital as a whole." Marx aims for an understanding of the movements of capital to provide a solution to the contradiction between the rate of profit (s/s + v) and the rate of surplus value (s/v) consistent with the law of value established in Volume One.

Part I is concerned with the formation of the rate of profit, still abstracted from the effect of the capital market. In this part, Marx introduces the concept of *cost-price* as it appears to the capitalist, and likewise, *price of production.*

Part II addresses the formation of the uniform rate of profit by means of taking the total social capital as a single whole as an analytical device.

> In this entire first part, we presume the amount of profit falling to a given capital to be equal to the total amount of surplus-value produced by means of this capital during a certain period of circulation. We thus leave aside for the present the fact that, on the one hand, this surplus-value may be broken up into various sub-forms, such as interest on capital, ground-rent, taxes, etc., and that, on the other, it is not, as a rule, identical with profit as appropriated by virtue of a general rate of profit, which will be discussed in the second part.
>
> MARX, 1894, Chapter 3

3.1.1 Chapter 1. Cost-Price and Profit

In Volume One Part I, Marx considered a bourgeois society in which independent producers exchanged the products of their own labour at their value. For the remainder of Volume One and in Volume Two, *capitalist* production was considered, but the units of capital were still taken in isolation from one another, exchanging the products of wage-labour at their value as independent producers. Both of these formations were analytical abstractions, but self-evidently they have a real basis in the history of bourgeois society.

In Volume Three, "the capitalist is the actual producer of the commodity," and the *whole social capital flows between the units of capital* according to its own laws. Only now do we have a representation of capitalism as it is, characterised by capital which is part of the capital market.

Just as the value of the product of independent producers with their own means of production is that of the ingredients consumed plus *their own labour-time*, "the capitalist cost of the commodity is measured by the expenditure of capital." This fact, well-known to everyday consciousness, is now introduced into the conceptual synthesis, without displacing the principle that value is determined by abstract labour-time.

For the capitalist, the cost of the ingredients consumed is the constant capital plus wages paid, although "the distinction between constant and variable capital has disappeared." The capitalist is only concerned with the total capital expended and "in its assumed capacity of offspring of the aggregate advanced capital, surplus-value takes the converted form of *profit*."

> In capitalist economics the cost-price assumes the false appearance of a category of value production itself.
>
> op. cit.

The commodity's value is thus this *cost of production* plus the surplus value, the unpaid labour appropriated from the labourer by the capitalist, now counted by the capitalist under the heading of profit.

If commodities are exchanged at their value, *all else being equal* (notably the composition of capital), this value will be realised as the price of the commodity – the *price of production*.

Thus Marx has framed the transactions as they appear to the capitalist, but with the composition held constant so that there is no contradiction with the findings made hitherto arise.

In this way, he has set the scene for the solution of the universally recognised problem of the contradiction between the rates of surplus value and profit, namely, that the rate of profit does not vary in proportion to the labour-power employed by an individual capital but solely in proportion to the total capital advanced.

At this point Marx points out that so long as a commodity is sold at a price greater than its cost-price, the capitalist makes a profit. Business will only come to a stand-still if the price of production falls below the cost of production. But the phenomenon of competition which regulates the general rate of profit can result in commodities being sold at below their *values*. Here Marx is pointing *not* to the accidental variations in selling price which always approximate value, but on the contrary connects the possibility of price differing from value according to "fundamentals laws" of capitalism. In this he is anticipating what is to follow in Part II.

3.1.2 Chapter 2. The Rate of Profit

In this chapter, Marx reflects on the complexity of the processes which determine the profit a capitalist realises on his capital which obscure the real origin of profit from surplus value.

3.1.3 Chapter 3. The Relation of Rate of Profit to Rate of Surplus-Value

In this chapter, Marx enumerates the factors which have a determining influence on c, v and s – the constant, variable and surplus value.

First, the value of money is assumed to be constant throughout.

Second, the period of turnover is left out of consideration for the present.

Third, the productivity of labour may vary from one unit of capital to another for a variety of reasons.

Fourth, the length of the working-day, intensity of labour, and wage levels.

Marx then illustrates how the components of value vary as a function of the above factors, as already established in Volumes One and Two.

3.1.4 Chapter 4. The Effect of the Turnover on the Rate of Profit

Here Marx examines the effect of turnover (time) on the components of value.

3.1.5 Chapter 5. Economy in the Employment of Constant Capital

This chapter reviews various ways in which the constant capital can be employed in a way which increase the rate of profit. First among these is the lengthening of the working day, but also the recycling of waste product, the economies of scale and such like.

3.1.6 Chapter 6. The Effect of Price Fluctuations

Again, Marx works through particulars, the principles of which have already been established in Volumes One and Two.

3.1.7 Chapter 7. Supplementary Remarks

Here Marx sums up the multiplicity of factors which contribute to the profit which a capitalist realises, particularly the appearance that profit originates in the process of circulation. All this contributes to the inability of the capitalists or their theoretical spokespeople to see that profit arises from unpaid labour-time.

Part I adds nothing new to what has already been determined in principle in Volumes One and Two, but simply points to the myriad of particular circumstances which obscure the essential truth of the origin of surplus value. And all this before he goes on the show that in reality, the absolute values of profit and surplus value appropriated by a single capital do not in principle coincide.

But in the meantime, Marx has introduced the concepts of *cost of production* and *price of production*, economic categories which Marx describes as "false appearances," but nonetheless appearances *for the capitalist*.

3.2 *Part II. Conversion of Profit into Average Profit*

3.2.1 Chapter 8. Different Compositions of Capitals in Different Branches of Production and Resulting Differences in Rates of Profit

> What we previously regarded as changes occurring successively with one and the same capital is now to be regarded as simultaneous differences among capital investments existing *side by side* in different spheres of production. In these circumstances we shall have to analyse: 1) the difference in the organic composition of capitals, and 2) the difference in their period of turnover.
>
> MARX, 1894, Chapter 8

Marx demonstrates the already well-established fact that if commodities are sold at their value, then capitals having different value composition, i.e., ratios of constant to variable capital, will enjoy different rates of profit, on the assumption that wages and the working day are the same across different industries. Differences in the rate of turnover will affect the rate of profit in different sectors in the same way.

> It would seem, therefore, that here the theory of value is incompatible with the actual process, incompatible with the real phenomena of production, and that for this reason any attempt to understand these phenomena should be given up.
>
> op. cit.

Having thus posed in clear terms the problem which arises from the assumption of a labour theory of value, Marx now proceeds to a solution.

3.2.2 Chapter 9. Formation of a General Rate of Profit (Average Rate of Profit) and Transformation of the Values of Commodities into Prices of Production

Marx approached this problem by first supposing that several capitals of equal magnitude trading in different sectors of the economy with different value-composition of capital be taken to be parts of a single capital. The surplus value appropriated by that joint capital is then shared equally among the different capitals, thus returning a uniform rate of profit despite the fact that each component has generated a different share of that surplus value. This corresponds to the capitalist ethos in which equality of human labour has been replaced by equality of capital, which is manifested in the institution of share-holding in capitalist companies.

The result is that in each case the price of the commodity produced is *above or below its value*, depending on whether the constant capital is below or above the average across the entire joint capital. If and only if the composition of capital in a sector is equal to the social average, then their products will be sold at their value.

Marx has turned the problem around. Under the rule of capital, a uniform rate of profit generates commodities whose *price* (systematically) *differs from their value*. Instead of the rate of profit being derived from the rate of surplus value, *price* is now to be derived from the rate of profit. Nevertheless,

> These particular rates of profit = s/C in every sphere of production, and must, as occurs in Part I of this volume, be deduced out of the values of the commodities. Without such deduction the general rate of profit (and consequently the price of production of commodities) remains a vague and senseless conception. Hence, the *price of production of a commodity is equal to its cost-price plus the profit*, allotted to it in per cent, in accordance with the general rate of profit, or, in other words, to its cost-price plus the average profit.
>
> op. cit.

No sense can be made of the average rate of profit without recourse to the labour theory of value which is required to determine the mass of surplus value which is available to be shared amongst the various capitals. The same circumstance prevails if the entire national economy is considered (except that the capitals will not necessarily be of equal size). Without it, the general rate of profit remains an arbitrary and inexplicable phenomenon.

Note that Marx has now defined the crucial concepts of *cost of production* and *price of production.* These are the crucial concepts which provide the driving force behind capital, even though they obscure the concept of value. These concepts are the objects of Part II of Volume Three. Their proportional difference now constitutes the rate of profit.

Volume One with its derivation of the value of commodities and the total value of surplus value available for distribution in the form of profit to the capitalist class remains an indispensible basis for the formation of the general rate of profit.

Thus the contradiction between the labour theory of value and the uniform rate of profit extant under capitalism does not result in the victory of the latter over the former and the eradication of the former, but rather the *sublation* of the former in the latter. Just as Hegel demonstrated time and again throughout the *Logic*. "The incompatibility is a mere assumption, an arbitrary assertion" (Hegel, 1831, §78). The task which Marx had to solve was *how* this compatibility is brought about.

> The rates of profit prevailing in the various branches of production are originally very different. These different rates of profit are equalized by competition to a single general rate of profit, which is the average of all these different rates of profit. The profit accruing in accordance with this general rate of profit to any capital of a given magnitude, whatever its organic composition, is called the average profit. The price of a commodity, which is equal to its cost-price *plus the share of the annual average profit* on the total capital invested (not merely consumed) in its production that falls to it in accordance with the conditions of turnover, is called its *price of production.*
>
> op. cit.

The competition referred to by Marx in the above excerpt refers to competition in the *capital* market which had not previously entered into consideration. Marx introduces this process by means of the device of taking capital to be a single entity which assigns a share of surplus value to its shareholders proportionately. However, Marx has introduced this by means of an analytical device and he has yet to demonstrate the *political-economic means* whereby shares are distributed among capitalists in proportion to the capital advanced.

The new concept of *price of production* includes a profit based on the total capital advanced instead of a surplus based on the variable capital expended and now expresses the appearance of the economic categories under capitalism.

Since the price of production includes the profit already realised when the product is sold to another capitalist, this profit is included as part of the cost-price of the buyer *not as profit*, and is included as part of the price of production of the end-product. The profits taken by the producers of all the component parts of a product (including the products consumed by the workers from their wages) add together as the share of profit in the end-product. Neither capitalist nor worker buy their requirements at value; only the average quota of profit will be included in price of any commodity, not the quota corresponding to the amount of variable and constant capital entailed in its production.

Thus, under capitalism every product contains a component of profit more or less equal in proportion to the capital invested, which has been appropriated by capitalists during its production. At the same time, every product contains a *variable* amount of surplus value, according to the unpaid labour appropriated. Therefore the price of a worker's wage, what is required for the purchase of their means of subsistence, will differ from the value of their labour power, just as does the products required by the capitalist for production. This means that a greater or less number of hours of unpaid labour will have to be appropriated by the capitalist every working day to cover the cost of wages. If the redistribution of surplus value between capitalists leads to an increase in the production price of the means of subsistence, this will have to be compensated by a loss of unpaid labour by the employer of those workers (assuming that workers are nevertheless paid enough to live and work for the prevailing working day, despite an increase in the necessary labour time).

> The general rate of profit is, therefore, determined by two factors:
>
> 1) The organic composition of the capitals in the different spheres of production, and thus, the different rates of profit in the individual spheres.
>
> 2) The *distribution* of the total social capital in these different spheres, and thus, the relative magnitude of the capital invested in each particular sphere at the specific rate of profit prevailing in it; i.e., the relative share of the total social capital absorbed by each individual sphere of production.
>
> op. cit.

First the total surplus appropriated is determined by the amount of abstract labour employed, and then its distribution among the capitalists is determined according to the general rate of profit set by the capital market.

Changes in the actual rate of profit occur continuously and the formation of a general rate of profit is only a "belated effect of a series of fluctuations extending over very long periods ... before consolidating and equalising one another to bring about a change in the general rate of profit." On the other hand, all changes in prices over shorter periods of time can be traced to actual changes in the conditions of production.

> Whatever the composition of an industrial capital ... it yields the same profit, given the same degree of labour exploitation and leaving aside individual differences, which, incidentally, disappear because we are dealing in both cases with the average composition of the entire sphere of production. The individual capitalist ... whose outlook is limited, rightly believes that his profit is not derived solely from the labour employed by him, or in his line of production. This is quite true, as far as his average profit is concerned. To what extent this profit is due to the aggregate exploitation of labour on the part of the total social capital, i. e., by all his capitalist colleagues – this interrelation is a complete mystery to the individual capitalist; all the more so, since no bourgeois theorists, the political economists, have so far revealed it.
>
> op. cit.

3.2.3 Chapter 10. Equalisation of the General Rate of Profit through Competition. Market-Prices and Market-Values. Surplus-Profit

Here Marx considers the case of a sphere of production where the value composition of capital happens to coincide with the social average composition (including both inputs and outputs). The price of production of commodities is therefore equal to their value, and the rate of profit is therefore already the same as the general rate of profit without any distribution of the surplus between capitals. "All other capitals, of whatever composition, tend toward this average under pressure of competition."

> The really difficult question is this: how is this equalization of profits into a general rate of profit brought about, since it is obviously a result rather than a point of departure?
>
> ...
>
> The whole difficulty arises from the fact that commodities are not exchanged simply as *commodities*, but as *products of capitals*, which claim participation in the total amount of surplus-value, proportional to

> their magnitude … And this claim is to be satisfied by the total price for commodities produced by a given capital in a certain space of time. This total price is, however, only the sum of the prices of the individual commodities produced by this capital.
>
> MARX, 1894, Chapter 10

That is, it is by means of the self-regulation of the price of commodities that the "sharing" of surplus value among capitalists is effected.

> Whatever the manner in which the prices of various commodities are first mutually fixed or regulated, their movements are always governed by the law of value. If the labour-time required for their production happens to shrink, prices fall; if it increases, prices rise, provided other conditions remain the same.
>
> op. cit.

This sharing takes place with a socially total amount of surplus value still determined according to the law of value.

> the values of commodities [is] not only theoretically but also historically *prius* to the prices of production. This applies to conditions in which the labourer owns his means of production, and this is the condition of the land-owning farmer living off his own labour and the craftsman, in the ancient as well as in the modern world.
>
> op. cit.

Marx says that the law of value is transhistorical. What varies is the manner of appropriation and distribution of the surplus. The law of value determines the value which *must* be allocated to the workers for their subsistence, and therefore the social total surplus value, and therefore the total profit. When labour is regarded from the standpoint of an entire economy which must distribute its labour among the various activities according to its needs, labour takes on the form of abstract labour which, however, exists as an actuality only in industrial capitalism.

Now Marx explicitly points to the mechanism which determines the sharing of surplus between capitals and brings about the equalisation of the rate of profit.

> it is competition of capitals in different spheres, which first brings out the price of production equalizing the rates of profit in the different spheres.
>
> op. cit.

What follows for the remainder of this chapter are Marx's observations on the regulation of prices by supply and demand. The only point which is relevant to his main line of argument is that:

> to say that a commodity has a use-value is merely to say that it satisfies some social want. So long as we dealt with individual commodities only, we could assume that there was a need for a particular commodity – its quantity already implied by its price without inquiring further into the quantity required to satisfy this want. This quantity is, however, of essential importance, as soon as the product of an entire branch of production is placed on one side, and the social need for it on the other. It then becomes necessary to consider the extent, i.e., the amount of this social want.
>
> op. cit.

Although, self-evidently the limit to the amount of the "social want" are elastic, the finitude of the social want has to be placed alongside the limits of the available social capital. Consequently, some social mechanism must exist which ensures the allocation of social labour so as to meet social wants. This fact comes into play in Chapter 12.

3.2.4 Chapter 11. Effects of General Wage Fluctuations on Prices of Production

In this chapter, Marx observes on the effect of wage fluctuations, but no new principles are introduced in the chapter.

3.2.5 Chapter 12. Supplementary Remarks

Here Marx addresses the operation of the capital market which is the means whereby the equalisation of the rate of profit is brought about.

> It has been said that competition levels the rates of profit of the different spheres of production into an average rate of profit and thereby turns the values of the products of these different spheres into prices of production. This occurs through the continual transfer of capital from one sphere to another, in which, for the moment, the profit happens to lie above average. ... This incessant outflow and inflow of capital between the different spheres of production creates trends of rise and fall in the rate of profit, which equalise one another more or less and thus have a tendency to reduce the rate of profit everywhere to the same common and general level.
>
> MARX, 1894, Chapter 12

Although the mechanism is the capital market:

> This movement of capitals is primarily caused by the level of market-prices [of products], which lift profits above the general average in one place and depress them below it in another.
>
> op. cit.

The flow of capital from one sector to another in the capital market and the flow of money through the market in commodities together establish the general rate of profit in each sector, whatever the composition of capital.

> What competition does *not* show, however, is the determination of value, which dominates the movement of production; and the values that lie beneath the prices of production and that determine them in the last instance.
>
> op. cit.

Thus, the capitalist's belief that he is entitled to a certain profit based on the total capital he advanced is vindicated by the operation of the capital market and the market in commodities – the conception that "every individual capital should be regarded merely as a part of the total social capital, and every capitalist actually as a shareholder in the total social enterprise, each sharing in the total profit pro rata to the magnitude of his share of capital." The capitalist does his calculations on this basis and the market confirms his wisdom, a prejudice shared by his brother capitalists.

This concludes the main problems which *Capital* was designed to address, so it is worth dwelling for a moment on the mechanism which Marx believes brings about the general rate of profit, while preserving the rate of surplus value as the chief determinant of the rate of profit.

Imagine that every capital appearing in the economy and momentarily fixing the prices of its products with the aim of maximising their own profit while limited by the prevailing technology in their sector and the length of the working day and average level intensity of the prevailing labour.

Firstly, all those capitals competing within the market for the same use-value are subject to competition with each other and this process fixes the price of the commodities and optimum technical means of production used and thereby fixes the rate of profit, equalised across this sector, whilst the rate of surplus value remain as ever at (s/v). Hereafter we can consider this sector as if it were a single capital allocating shares of profit according to capital invested.

Secondly, this capital finds itself working alongside other sectors providing other use-values with a different rate of profit. The capital market puts each of these capitals in competition with each other, enticing capital by offering a rate of profit, and capital accordingly *moves* from one sector to another in pursuit of profit. Only so much value can be invested in each sector (although the limits are elastic) consequently, supply and demand will push market prices above or below the value of commodities so as to equalise the rate of profit in each sector.

In effect, this amounts to capital in one sector which employs a high proportion of labour relative to the amount of capital advanced *cross-subsidising* those sectors with a relatively large proportion of constant capital to sustain. This is the mechanism whereby the commodity market combines with the capital market (and the labour market) to bring the prices of commodities in line with the ethos of capital which demands that the price of commodities reflect the amount of capital invested in their production.

The following observation which appears in Chapter 15 is apt:

> So long as things go well, competition effects an operating fraternity of the capitalist class, as we have seen in the case of the equalisation of the general rate of profit, so that each shares in the common loot in proportion to the size of his respective investment. But as soon as it no longer is a question of sharing profits, but of sharing losses, everyone tries to reduce his own share to a minimum and to shove it off upon another. The class, as such, must inevitably lose. How much the individual capitalist must bear of the loss, *i.e.*, to what extent he must share in it at all, is decided by strength and cunning, and competition then becomes a fight among hostile brothers. The antagonism between each individual capitalist's interests and those of the capitalist class as a whole, then comes to the surface, just as previously the identity of these interests operated in practice through competition.
>
> MARX, 1894, Chapter 15

3.3 *Part III. The Law of the Tendency of the Rate of Profit to Fall*

The unspoken agenda in all of Marx's work on political economy is to locate a possible source of capitalism's final crisis. Far from *Capital* presenting a closed logical system, like Hegel, Marx always sought that moment of indeterminacy where the system can no longer provide an answer to the questions which the system itself has asked. Any secular historical tendency in a system is bound to lead to a crisis at some point. Marx believed he had found this Achilles' heel in the "tendency of the rate of profit to fall."

3.3.1 Chapter 13. The Law as Such

Marx shows that:

> the gradual growth of constant capital in relation to variable capital must necessarily lead to *a gradual fall of the general rate of profit.*
>
> MARX, 1894, Chapter 13

This tendency is

> just *an expression peculiar to the capitalist mode of production* of the progressive development of the social productivity of labour.
>
> op. cit.

which Marx has observed always entails an increase in constant capital, both investment in plant and for the cost of materials consumed by ever more productive labour. This secular tendency for the increasing productivity of labour, deriving from the unceasing drive of each capital to increase their profit, leads inevitably to a disproportion between the values of means of production to that of the labour-power employed in the production process and a consequent *fall* in the rate of profit.

Marx reasons that the process of capital accumulation will never lack for a mass of labour power available for exploitation, and that while the absolute mass of surplus value will increase, even with an increase in wages, the *rate* of surplus value will tend to decline. The fall in the rate of profit co-exists with an ever-increasing rate of surplus value and consequently the ever-growing mass of capital accumulated every year.

The root cause of this tendency is the tendency capitalism to drive up *relative surplus value*, and "a disproportion between the progressive growth of capital and its relatively shrinking need for an increasing population."

Thus capitalism faces an historical tendency which both concentrates a larger proportion of the wealth of society in ever fewer hands and produces a decline in the rate of profit which is the very thing which provides industrial capital with the motive force for its development.

3.3.2 Chapter 14. Counteracting Influences

Marx referred to the falling rate of profit as a "tendency" rather than a "law" because he recognised a number of countervailing influences, namely:

Increasing intensity of exploitation, by lengthening of the working day and intensification of labour, obviously subject to finite limits;

Depression of wages below the value of labour power, though this tendency is also subject to definite limits;

Cheapening of the elements of constant capital – just as the increasing productivity of labour reduces the necessary labour time for the worker, it can also reduce the labour time necessary for the production of the means of production. Thus the *value* of the constant capital will grow, but not grow as fast as its material volume;

Relative over-population, which can furnish newly developing industries with abundant labour. This tendency is necessarily transient however;

Foreign trade, increasing the rate of surplus value and cheapening the supply of constant capital, especially raw materials, and the opportunity to sell in markets where industry is unable to compete with modern capitalist methods and thereby reap super-profits. In the long run these tendencies are cancelled out by the spread of capitalist development internationally.

Increase of capital in the form of stocks and shares which, because of the progress of capital accumulation, becomes larger and larger in relation to the mass of productive capital absorbing an ever-growing portion of the share of profits accruing to industrial capital. Thus a larger and larger mass of capital demanding its share of the proceeds of industrial capital.

Present-day Marxist research confirms Marx's insight:

> According to the estimates presented in this book [Moseley, 1991], the trends in the Marxian variables were largely consistent with Marx's hypotheses that the rate of profit would tend to decline due to technological change. The Marxian rate of profit declined for the reason suggested by Marx's theory: because the composition of capital increased faster than the rate of surplus-value. This conclusion is strengthened by a consideration of the effects of "other factors" (the distribution of capital, the turnover of capital, and multiple shifts) on the rate of profit. These "other factors" all had significant positive effects on the rate of profit, which implies that technological change by itself had an even greater negative effect on the rate of profit than my estimates show.
>
> LAIBMAN, 1993, p. 152

3.3.3 Chapter 15. Exposition of the Internal Contradictions of the Law

The reasons which cause Marx to see this tendency as the site of contradictions, that is to say, "impossible situations" for capitalism, are as follows.

The first contradiction which Marx identifies is that of over-production of commodities unable to be paid for by an impoverished population. "The conditions of direct exploitation, and those of realising it, are not identical," made acute by the "antagonistic conditions of distribution, which reduce the consumption of the bulk of society to a minimum." One cannot avoid observing that this tendency places a powerful weapon in the hands of the workers' movement when it struggles to raise the living standards of the working population.

Marx also discusses at length the phenomena which result from this process which Marx sees as a secular process, i.e., it increases over time in the absence of any countervailing tendency in the system. These include the decline in the force which motivates capitalist development, the obliteration of small capitalist enterprises, and the suppression of new capitals, periodic crises of over-production – factors which lead to depression, the development of uncontrollable markets and sharpening conflicts of industrial capital with each other and with landed and finance capital, as well as expansion of parasitic finance capital.

The essence of the tendency remains however – the ever growing proportion of the value of the means of production, alongside a smaller proportion of that wealth accruing to the only sector of society which is generating profit, the working class. Having identified this universal principle, a vast array of particular problems arise and, while these are of great interest to economists, they have little to tell us in respect to Hegel's influence on *Capital*.

3.4 *Part IV. Conversion of Commodity-Capital and Money-Capital into Commercial Capital and Money-Dealing Capital (Merchant's Capital)*

Marx has already observed that surplus value originates from unpaid labour acquired by productive capital, which is in turn reproduced by means of circulation of value through the entire social formation. The costs of circulation must be paid out of the surplus. Likewise, all other sections of the capitalist class must gain their revenue at the cost of the surplus value directly appropriated by industrial capital. In Part IV, Marx examines this sharing of the social surplus acquired by productive capital among capitalists engaged in the business of circulation of commodity-capital. Again, Marx is following the method of moving from the universal to the particular.

3.4.1 Chapter 16. Commercial Capital

Marx divides "merchant's" capital into two types of unit: "commercial" capitals and "money-dealing" capitals – capital located in alternate phases of the circulation of commodity-capital.

In Volume Two on circulation, capital in the form of commodities and capital in the form of money are seen to be continuously converting into one another. Commercial capital is that capital which acquires its share of the surplus through involvement in this process of metamorphosis. "A special function of a special capital, as a function established by virtue of the division of labour to a special group of capitalists, commodity-capital becomes commercial capital."

Insofar as commercial capital bears the costs of circulation, transport, storage and distribution of commodities these functions "may be regarded as production processes continuing within the process of circulation." Marx, however, regards these activities as incidental to the nature of commercial capital in its "pure form," found when commercial capital is stripped of these activities which are either entirely absent or incidental to its existence. Commercial capital is continuously changing its form in the buying and selling of commodities, independently of its function in the actual circulation of productive capital.

Commercial capital begins as a sum of money; this money is transformed into commodities and back into money, returning with a profit, without ever having passed through any process of production or even packaging and transport. This is commercial capital in its *pure form.*

Conversely, the involvement of commercial capital in the transport of commodities and the necessary retail labour required to realise the commodity capital as money, is a necessary cost to surplus value and therefore a deduction from the surplus value, but it is not the essential business of commercial capital. The core business of commercial capital is the cornering a share of the surplus for itself, at the going rate of profit.

Commercial capital arises on the basis of a division of labour among capitalists, each being involved in a specific phase of the circulation of capital, namely, the conversion of commodities into money. It arises because this activity requires the initial advance of capital for the purchase of the products of productive capital, and consequently a specific section of capital finds its place in the social division of labour by advancing capital for this purpose. The money provided by the commercial capitalist is necessary to ensure the continuity of the activity of productive capital. Commercial capital exists only insofar as it is able to achieve this metamorphosis more quickly and more cheaply than the industrial capitalist herself who wants to continue the cycle of production as rapidly as possible and without interruption, rather than diverting capital towards distribution of the products. The velocity of turnover of capital is a crucial determinant of both the commercial capitalist and the industrial capitalist's profit.

> But no value is produced in the process of circulation, and, therefore, no surplus-value. ... If a surplus-value is realised in the sale of produced

> commodities, then this is only because it already existed in them. ... In so far as it contributes to shortening the time of circulation, it may help indirectly to increase the surplus-value produced by the industrial capitalists. In so far as it helps to expand the market and effects the division of labour between capitals.
>
> MARX, 1894, Chapter 16

The surplus value that commercial capital has appropriated is but a share of the surplus value originally appropriated by productive capital.

3.4.2 Chapter 17. Commercial Profit

> Since the circulation phase of industrial capital is just as much a phase of the reproduction process as production is, the capital operating independently in the process of circulation must yield the average annual profit just as well as capital operating in the various branches of production.
>
> MARX, 1894, Chapter 17

In this respect then, commercial capital participates in the sharing out of the social surplus value in the capital market like any sector of industrial capital, even though it adds to the appropriation of unpaid labour only incidentally. Accordingly, the commercial capital enters into the formation of the general rate of profit as a component part of the total capital advanced, alongside productive capital, thereby having the effect of *lowering the general rate of profit* so that it can take its share. This is the means by which commercial capital takes its profit as a share of the surplus attributed to the activity of productive capital.

It follows from this that the employees of the commercial capitalists, like those of the industrial capitalists, are paid wages determined by the value of the means of subsistence, but unlike the industrial worker, the commercial worker's wage is paid out of a portion of the surplus appropriated by commercial capital and does not itself generate surplus value. "The unpaid labour of these clerks, while it does not *create* surplus-value, enables him to appropriate surplus-value, which, in effect, amounts to the same thing with respect to his capital."

3.4.3 Chapter 18. The Turnover of Merchant's Capital. Prices

While constrained by the turnover time of productive capital on one side and by the short turnover time of individual consumption on the other, commercial capital is generally speaking able to turnover its capital more quickly, having only to replace commodities with commodities of the same kind in each cycle of reproduction. Its rapid turnover promotes the rate of turnover of industrial capital.

The value available for appropriation by commercial capital is constrained by the amount of surplus value created by productive capital and the going general rate of profit. All the commercial capitalist can do is maximize their share of trade, turn over their capital as fast as possible, run their business and set their prices to ensure that they get their share of the available surplus. But they have no overall effect on the prices of commodities, despite the appearance that it is they who are setting the prices.

3.4.4 Chapter 19. Money-Dealing Capital

Just as commercial capital is a special group of capitalists whose capital is engaged in the special function of the circulation of the products of productive capital and uses this position to corner a portion of the total social capital and enjoy the same general rate of profit, so

> A definite part of the total capital dissociates itself from the rest and stands apart in the form of money-capital, whose capitalist function consists exclusively in performing these operations [the purely technical movements performed by money in the circulation process] for the entire class of industrial and commercial capitalists.
>
> MARX, 1894, Chapter 19

That section of capital which is engaged in the purely technical business of facilitating the circulation of capital, like commercial capital, receive only a share of the surplus which can be skimmed off during circulation. Just as in the case of commercial capital, on the basis of seeing to the technical matter of transforming commodities into money and vice versa, money-dealing capital expands into kindred activity.

On the other hand,

> when, and in so far as, capital is newly invested ... capital in money-form appears as the starting-point and the end result of the movement.
>
> op. cit.

Chapter 20 is devoted to historical reflections on merchant's capital, noting that "not commerce alone, but also merchant's capital, is older than the capitalist mode of production, is, in fact, historically the oldest free state of existence of capital," and consequently has played a crucial role in the emergence of industrial capital. As a subject matter of *Capital*, however, its place is a subordinate one, while industrial capitalism is the focus of interest.

3.5 *Part v. Division of Profit into Interest and Profit of Enterprise: Interest-Bearing Capital*

The object of Part v is *finance capital*, that section of capital which enriches itself from the surplus value derived from interest through lending money-capital for the initiation of a productive enterprise by industrial capital. Finance capital arises out of money-dealing capital which originated in the circulation of commodity-capital, but it has a distinct life outside of the business of circulation of commodities. I use shall use the term "finance capital" synonymously with what Marx calls "interest-bearing capital."

In Part I of Volume One, the object was a simple commodity, the basic unit of a society of *independent producers*, exchanged at its value. Everything that we have seen from Part II of Volume One up to the immediately preceding Part IV has concerned *industrial capital*, with its individual unit M–C–M' personified by Moneybags, its particular sectors competing in commodity markets for the same use-value, and universal capital established through the circulation of capital examined in Volume Two. With consideration of the capital market, Volume Three has determined that the products of productive industrial capital are exchanged at their price of production, not their value.

In Part v of Volume Three, Marx moves to a new layer of industrial capitalism with a new ethos, distinct from that of productive capital – finance capital.

3.5.1 Chapter 21. Interest-Bearing Capital

The first step in this part will be to identify the unit, the universal individual unit of finance capital, the current object. It is the distinctive nature of this unit which distinguishes finance capital from industrial capital, which has hitherto been the subject matter.

> Since [the general rate of profit] is the same for mercantile, as well as industrial, capital, it is no longer necessary, so far as this average profit is concerned, to make a distinction between industrial and commercial profit. Whether industrially invested in the sphere of production, or commercially in the sphere of circulation, capital yields the same average annual profit *pro rata* to its magnitude.
>
> MARX, 1894, Chapter 21

It remains the case, however, that merchant's capital generates no surplus value and its activity can only contribute to distributing the surplus obtained by productive capital amongst the various sections of the capitalist class.

The distinctive universal function of the class of *finance* capitalists is the advance of money capital to initiate new productive enterprises.

> [Money's] use-value then consists precisely in the profit it produces when converted into capital. In this capacity of potential capital, as a means of producing profit, it becomes a commodity, but a commodity *sui generis*. Or, what amounts to the same, capital as capital becomes a commodity.
>
> op. cit.

This commodity is referred to as the *capital-commodity*.

The embryonic, universal individual capital which we met in Part II of Volume One, M–C–M', and the universal form of circulation which we met in Part I of Volume Two, M–C ... P ... C'–M', both begin not with saving by the productive capitalist, but with an advance to the industrialist from finance capital for whom it is their special business: M–M–C ... P ... C'–M'–M'

With finance capital, capital itself is a commodity. This is called the capital-commodity. Its universal form is that of the money ("potential capital") advanced to financial institution with the expectation of receiving interest. In the course of its circuit, productive capital is transformed into commodity-capital and money-capital and back to productive capital. These forms of capital are distinct from this form in which capital is a commodity *qua* capital. The peculiar manner in which interest-bearing capital is sold as a commodity, is that *it is loaned instead of relinquished once and for all*. Like labour-power, its use-value lies in its *use* by productive capital, not its ownership, and it remains the property of the seller throughout the productive process.

The augmented capital which is returned to the lender, M' or M + ΔM, is not the whole profit obtained by use of M in some enterprise, but only the interest on M. ΔM is the share of the surplus value extracted by productive capital which is paid ultimately to the individual lender, at which point it ceases to act as capital. The lender remains the legal owner of the advanced capital throughout. A finance capital institution mediates this transfer of interest to the lender. The remainder of ΔM after interest is paid is retained by the productive capitalist.

Marx here reminds us of the distinction between commodity-capital and an ordinary commodity (as found in Chapter 1 of Volume One): commodity-capital contains a portion of surplus value which is realised on sale, as part of reproduction of the producer's capital. The same distinction applies to money-capital which exists within the cycle of reproduction of industrial capital in the form of means of payment, distinct from money advanced by finance capital. The specific nature of capital *as capital*, and therefore as a capital-commodity, depends on its position within the cycle of reproduction of capital, namely, the *initiation* of capitalist enterprises.

Marx says that commodities, such as houses, ships, ... may be loaned as capital which "is always only a *particular* form of money-capital." The reflux of loaned capital, whatever the form of that capital, is always in the form of payments in money. But the universal form of capital is money-capital, here in the form of a capital-commodity, and it is this form alone which is treated in this chapter. According to the Hegelian conception, the universal form, money, exists alongside particular forms, such as infrastructure.

When money is advanced as capital and is put into circulation to return in an expanded quantity, it is ready to perform the same process over again.

> This relation to itself, in which capital presents itself when the capitalist production process is viewed as a whole and as a single unity, and in which capital appears as money that begets money, is here imparted to it as its character, its designation, without any intermediary movement. And it is relinquished with this designation when loaned out as money-capital.
>
> op. cit.

The return of interest-bearing capital to its point of departure differs from the circuit of other forms of capital in that it is transferred to the industrial capitalist without receiving any equivalent and ownership is not relinquished. The borrower *must* return the money with interest to the lender irrespective of whether or not he has made any use of the money at all.

> The bare *form* of capital – money expended as a certain sum, A, which returns as sum A + 1/x A after a given lapse of time without any other intermediate act save this lapse of time – is only a meaningless form of the actual movement of capital.
>
> op. cit.

It is only this act of handing over money which changes lending money into alienation of money as capital, *i.e.*, alienation of *capital as a commodity*, "potential capital." The finance capitalist, in fact, alienates a use-value, and thus whatever he gives away is given as a commodity. The use-value is the profit obtained by its use *as capital*. The buyer pays for this use-value at its value, the profit which can be made by its use as capital. On the other hand, not *all* the profit can fall to the lender's share, for in that case the capital would be useless to the borrower.

> Interest, signifying the price of capital, is from the outset quite an irrational expression.
>
> op. cit.

Where capital appears as a commodity, it is subject to the laws of supply and demand. But whereas in the case of all other commodities, there is a *value* underlying the fluctuations caused by the momentary imbalance of supply and demand. In the case of interest, "there is no law of division except that enforced by competition, because, as we shall later see, no such thing as a 'natural' rate of interest exists." This is dealt with in the next chapter.

To reiterate, Marx has introduced a process distinct from industrial capital dealt with in all the preceding parts of *Capital*, *finance capital*. Its unit is the capital-commodity, a possibly quite small sum of money loaned as potential capital to some financial institution for use as capital. The lender is paid for use of the potential capital with interest at an agreed rate, irrespective of the use made of the money. This entire transaction lies *outside* of the cycle of reproduction of industrial capital.

The total financial capital across an economy constitutes the *universal* finance capital, each financial institution is a particular unit of finance capital, its smallest unit being the deposit made by an agent at a financial institution.

3.5.2 Chapter 22. Division of Profit. Rate of Interest. Natural Rate of Interest

According to Marx, the average rate of profit is to be regarded as the ultimate determinant of the maximum limit of interest, but there is no such thing as a 'natural' rate of interest. Even in Marx's day, interest rates were influenced by international movements of capital and the interventions of central banks. Marx was not able to finally determine the setting of the rate of interest other than its still-elastic limits, which determine the sharing of surplus value between finance capital and industrial capital.

3.5.3 Chapter 23. Interest and Profit of Enterprise

Capital loaned out remains the property of the lender, who receives interest payments at regular intervals for its use. Should the lender withdraw the capital, it ceases to function as capital until it is invested again and tied up with the cycle of industrial capital.

> It is indeed only the separation of capitalists into money-capitalists and industrial capitalists that transforms a portion of the profit into interest, that generally creates the category of interest; and it is only the competition between these two kinds of capitalists which creates the rate of interest. … The employer of capital, even when working with his own capital, splits into two personalities – the owner of capital and the employer of capital.
>
> MARX, 1894, Chapter 23

The division of gross profit into interest and profit of enterprise becomes, not merely a quantitative division of the proceeds, but a *qualitative* one.

> To represent functioning capital is not a sinecure, like representing interest-bearing capital. On the basis of capitalist production, the capitalist directs the process of production and circulation. Exploiting productive labour entails exertion, whether he exploits it himself or has it exploited by someone else on his behalf. Therefore, his profit of enterprise appears to him as distinct from interest, as independent of the ownership of capital, but rather as the result of his function as a non-proprietor – a *labourer*. … the industrial capitalist, as distinct from the owner of capital, does not appear as operating capital, but rather as a functionary irrespective of capital, or, as a simple agent of the labour-process in general, as a labourer, and indeed as a wage-labourer.
>
> op. cit.

The labour of the exploiting and the exploited labour both appear identical as labour. The social form of capital falls to interest. The economic function of an industrial capitalist, like "that of an orchestra conductor," is to ensure the profit of an enterprise.

> The industrial capitalist is a worker, compared to the money-capitalist, but a worker in the sense of capitalist, *i.e.*, an exploiter of the labour of others. The wage which he claims and pockets for this labour is exactly equal to the appropriated quantity of another's labour and depends directly upon the rate of exploitation of this labour, in so far as he undertakes the effort required for exploitation.
>
> op. cit.

With the development of a numerous class of industrial and commercial managers, many of them former industrial capitalists, the wages of supervision, like any other wage, find their definite level and definite market-price.

Thus, it is in interest-bearing capital that we find capital in its purest form.

3.5.4 Chapter 24. Externalisation of the Relations of Capital in the Form of Interest-Bearing Capital

> The relations of capital assume their most externalised and most *fetish-like* form in interest-bearing capital. We have here M – M', money creating more money, self-expanding value, without the process that effectuates these two extremes. ... The social relation is consummated in the relation ... of money to itself
>
> MARX, 1894, Chapter 24

For the remainder of this chapter, Marx illustrates the mystique that interest-bearing capital engenders in money with quotes from numerous sources, both ancient and modern,

3.5.5 Chapter 25. Credit and Fictitious Capital

Here Marx explores the basis of bank-notes, which he says arise from "bills of exchange" created by commercial capitalists to facilitate exchange of commodities with each other. These bills have value only until the exchange is completed after which they become redundant. Alongside this activity of commercial capital, there is international monetary exchange and the operation of the credit system. In the course of this activity, banks, as a special class of capitalists, come to centralise the activity of all the lenders, on one hand, and all the borrowers on the other. A portion of the money circulating as commercial capital is turned to use as interest-bearing capital. In the course of this business, banks issue credit notes themselves as promissory notes against the bank itself. The continuous movement of credit through the banks places banks in a position to issue credit beyond the capital they hold at any given moment.

Chapter 26, "Accumulation of Money-Capital. Its Influence on the Interest Rate," is composed of a review of contemporary discourse about the relation between interest rates and the circulation of bank-notes.

3.5.6 Chapter 27. The Role of Credit in Capitalist Production

The credit system functions to effect the equalisation of the rate of profit, reduce the costs of circulation by removing altogether the need for many transactions, accelerating circulation, the substitution of paper money for gold, and the formation of stock companies.

In joint stock companies:

> The capital, which in itself rests on a social mode of production and presupposes a social concentration of means of production and labour-power, is here directly endowed with the form of social capital (capital of directly associated individuals) as distinct from private capital, and its undertakings assume the form of social undertakings as distinct from private undertakings. It is the abolition of capital as private property within the framework of capitalist production itself.
>
> MARX, 1894, Chapter 27

Joint stock companies enable production on a large scale, beyond what is possible with private capital at a given point in its development. The actually functioning capitalist is here fully transformed into a mere manager, an administrator of other people's capital, and paid an appropriate salary.

Function is entirely divorced from ownership.

Profit now assumes the pure form of interest.

> This is the abolition of the capitalist mode of production within the capitalist mode of production itself, and hence a self-dissolving contradiction, which *prima facie* represents a mere phase of transition to a new form of production.
>
> op. cit.

By means of large stock companies, the capitalist is able to control large masses of social capital, no longer just his own capital. Social property is appropriated by a few.

> The credit system appears as the main lever of over-production and over-speculation in commerce solely because the reproduction process, which is elastic by nature, is here forced to its extreme limits.
>
> op. cit.

Here Marx seems to be alluding back to the passage in Volume One where the "expropriators are expropriated." The joint stock company appears as the terminal form of capital with the capitalist making no contribution to social production which is already organised as an integral system.

At the same time, the credit system is "the purest and most colossal form of gambling and swindling, and reduces more and more the number of the few who exploit the social wealth; on the other hand, to constitute the form of transition to a new mode of production."

Chapter 28 is devoted to a critique of the views of Tooke and Fullaraton.

Chapter 29, "Component Parts of Bank Capital," dwells on the distinction between money serving as capital in circulation and actual money-capital.

3.5.7 Chapter 30–35. Money-Capital and Real Capital

In these chapters Marx seeks to understand the relation of the various forms of credit to *real* capital, that is, commodity-capital, productive capital and money-capital involved in the circuit of productive capital. He asks "to what extent does the accumulation of capital in the form of loanable money-capital coincide with actual accumulation"?

> These promissory notes, which are issued for the originally loaned capital long since spent, these paper duplicates of consumed capital, serve for their owners as capital to the extent that they are saleable commodities … titles to real capital. … likewise become paper duplicates of the real capital … nominally represent non-existent capital.
>
> MARX, 1894, Chapter 30

The essential form of all these forms of paper money is "money loans, which are made by bankers, as middlemen, to industrialists and merchants." In this capacity, initiating the cycle of reproduction of capital, credit plays an essential function in capitalism.

However, Marx begins his analysis with a consideration of credit extended from one commercial or industrial capitalist to another, purely commercial credit. He sees bank credit as an outgrowth of credit arising from its necessary function within the circuit of reproduction of industrial and commercial capital. The social need for these credit notes was to maintain the continuity of reproduction despite interruptions and the effect of the business cycle.

Since the same capital gathered from the circulation of commercial and productive capital can be loaned and re-loaned multiple times, the mass of credit can far outweigh the mass of actual capital which underwrites it. So long as there are no interruptions to circulation, all can function as claims for interest on others. Consequently, "a large portion of this money-capital is always necessarily purely fictitious, that is, a title to value" which duplicates other such titles.

Marx frequently makes use of terms like "unintelligible," "incomprehensible" and "irrational." While citing reams of text from bourgeois commentators and mocking their illusions, Marx is able to point to various effects on the value of this paper-money, but little clarity emerges from his considerations. Questions still remain about the meaning of "real" and "fictitious" capital.

Part V concludes with:

3.5.8 Chapter 36. Pre-capitalist Relationships

> Interest-bearing capital, or, as we may call it in its antiquated form, usurer's capital, belongs together with its twin brother, merchant's capital, to the antediluvian forms of capital, which long precede the capitalist mode of production and are to be found in the most diverse economic formations of society.
>
> MARX, 1894, Chapter 36

Marx argues that the extent to which the accumulation of large amounts of money-capital by usurers can bring about the ruin of large-scale landholders and the impoverishment of small producers, opening the way for capitalism, as happened in modern Europe, depends on "the stage of historical development." Usurer's capital and merchant's wealth promotes the formation of moneyed wealth independent of landed property.

The credit system develops as a reaction against usury.

> What distinguishes interest-bearing capital – in so far as it is an essential element of the capitalist mode of production – from usurer's capital is … merely the altered conditions under which it operates, as a part of the cycle of reproduction of productive capital.
>
> op. cit.

3.6 *Part VI. Transformation of Surplus-Profit into Ground-Rent*

The object of Part VI is *rent*: that portion of surplus value which is appropriated in the form of ground-rent under conditions of modern industrial capitalism.

3.6.1 Chapter 37. Introduction

> The analysis of landed property in its various historical forms is beyond the scope of this work. We shall be concerned with it only in so far as a portion of the surplus-value produced by capital falls to the share of the landowner. We assume, then, that agriculture is dominated by the capitalist mode of production just as manufacture is; in other words, that agriculture is carried on by capitalists who differ from other capitalists primarily in the manner in which their capital, and the wage-labour set in motion by this capital, are invested.
>
> MARX, 1894, Chapter 37

Capitalism dissolves the connection between the landowner and the land so that landed property adopts its purely economic form without any of the traditional accessories of landownership. This opens the land (and water) to the conscious application of capitalist methods of operation with the use of wage-labour, like any other element of the means of production.

Capital invested in improvement of the land belongs to the category of fixed capital. Interest on capital so invested constitutes part of the rent paid by the capitalist farmer to the landowner, even when this investment is in fact made by the farmer – a practice which obviously discourages a tenant farmer from making any such improvement which does not bring immediate gain. Not only does this investment increase the value of the land, but the value of the land also increases with the general cultural and economic development of the surrounding area from whatever source – the presence of transport infrastructure, population centres, etc. – in which the landowner plays no part.

Ground-rent paid by the capitalist farmer to the landowner is paid out of the surplus value extracted through the use of labour-power on the land. That part of the value of a product which is accounted for by rent is part of the surplus value, and the general rate of profit will be applicable to the capitalist farmer as for any other capitalist.

If the land is purchased, its price is determined jointly by its potential for generating rent and the going rate of interest, and the portion of the value of the product so determined remains a part of the surplus value created by the exploitation of wage-labour by productive capital.

3.6.2 Chapter 38–44. Differential Rent

Differential rent is the rent for land which has some particular quality which is beneficial for its productive use. It arises through the claim to a super-profit gained by the capitalist user of the land, it being assumed that the general rate of profit will determine the price of production prevailing in a given market.

3.6.3 Chapter 45. Absolute Ground-Rent

Only such land pays ground-rent whose product has an individual price of production below the price of production regulating the market. However, the "absolute" rent which even the worst land can, under certain conditions, yield is the result of the monopoly of land by the class of landowners. The room for this "tax" upon the capitalist farmer or miner derives from the fact that the value of the product of the agricultural sector may be greater than would otherwise be the price of production. Normally, this results in a redistribution of surplus-value to other sector whose composition of capital otherwise leads to a lower rate of profit.

> Given the same rate of surplus-value, … equally large capitals in various spheres of production produce different amounts of surplus-value, in

> accordance with their varying average composition. In industry these various masses of surplus-value are equalised into an average profit and distributed uniformly among the individual capitals as aliquot parts of the social capital. Landed property hinders such an equalisation among capitals, invested in land, whenever production requires land for either agriculture or extraction of raw materials, and takes hold of a portion of the surplus-value, which would otherwise take part in equalising to the general rate of profit. The rent, then, forms a portion of the value, or, more specifically, surplus-value, of commodities, and instead of falling into the lap of the capitalists, who have extracted it from their labourers, it falls to the share of the landlords, who extract it from the capitalists.
>
> MARX, 1894, Chapter 45

3.6.4 Chapter 46. Building Site Rent. Rent in Mining. Price of Land

Having established the universal principles of rent from consideration of agricultural land, Marx moves to particular uses of land.

In such cases, it is the presence nearby development and services which give to the person who has the privilege of being the owner of the land the leverage to extract from the user of the land a charge based on their monopoly position.

Chapter 47 is devoted to historical reflections on capitalist ground-rent.

3.6.5 Summary of Parts V and VI

Like the interest paid to financial capital out of the surplus extracted from the working class by productive capital, the rent paid to landowning class is paid as a cost to surplus value.

The quantity of rent obtained by the landowner has two components. (1) "Differential rent" which derives from the particular contribution to profit of enterprise resulting from some natural advantage possessed by the particular piece of land or advantages resulting from economic development in the neighbourhood; (2) "Absolute rent" which the landowning class can extract from the capitalist by means of its monopoly. This component is obtained by diverting a portion of the surplus value transferred to the relevant sector due to the low level of variable capital and consequent low rate of surplus value in the sector. It is always constrained by the general rate of profit prevailing across the whole economy. Were a monopoly rate of rent to be applied which would lift the production price of the product above the market level, then production would stop.

Part VI clarifies a number of issues arising from what has gone before, including Marx's only analysis of competition, though more an explanation of why no analysis of competition is necessary. For example, on the formation of the general rate of profit "by competition," Marx remarks:

> In order to equalise unequal rates of profit, profit must exist as an element in the price of commodities. Competition does not create it. It lowers or raises its level, but does not create the level which is established when equalisation has been achieved.
>
> MARX, 1894, Chapter 2

The same observations apply to the formation of prices and the increase of labour productivity and reduction of necessary labour time in Volume One.

CHAPTER 3

Overview and Reflections

1 Marx's *Capital*: Overview

The aim of this overview is to explicitly present the *structure* of Marx's *Capital.*

1.1 *The Division of the Material by Forms of Ethical Life*

In lieu of the rights-bearing person, the moral subject and the citizen of Hegel's *Philosophy of Right, Capital* presents the capitalist economy in three conflicting layers each of which is a specific economic ethos, each an analytical abstraction which has logical, historical and social basis. This three-layer structure does not correspond to the division of the work into three volumes.

1.1.1 Bourgeois Society

In Bourgeois Society, independent producers (individuals or companies) own their own means of production and exchange their products at their value, that is, according to the average labour-time required for the production of each commodity. One commodity singles itself out to play the role of a universal equivalent, namely money. The producers do not necessarily appropriate a surplus, and may stop work once they have produced the equivalent of the necessities for their subsistence.

This formation is presented in Part I of Volume One of *Capital.* Bourgeois society originated in the Middle Ages within the interstices of feudal society. guildmasters organised themselves in guilds and companies in which decisions were made on the basis of one man one vote. These guilds included both artisans and merchants.

Since people must labour whatever the social form of that labour and however the surplus labour is appropriated, this chapter establishes the meaning of "value" in its simplest social form, the commodity, and its magnitude as abstract labour-time.

1.1.2 Productive Capitalism

In Productive Capitalism, capitalist firms buy and sell their products as commodities, but the independent producers of bourgeois society have been split into capitalists and proletarians. The capitalists use labour-power purchased from the proletarians, who lack means of production, are paid a subsistence wage and are forced to work long hours, the surplus of which is appropriated by the capitalists.

It is only in Volume Three, Part II that we find that the capitalist firms sell their products not at value but at cost-price plus profit, profit being proportional to the total capital turned over in a given period of time.

Commercial capital develops as a branch of productive capital engaged in the technical business of the circulation of commodity-capital and its conversion into money-capital returning to production.

Productive capital is dealt with beginning with Part II of Volume One in which the embryonic unit of capital is defined, up to Part III of Volume III. Part IV deals with commercial capital, which exists side-by-side with industrial capital.

1.1.3 Finance Capital

Finance Capital arises out of commercial capital but is concerned only with the loaning of money-capital and trading in various forms of credit. The productive capitalist is essentially transformed into a salaried manager or supervisor of productive capital. Ownership is separated from function, and capital achieves its pure form lacking any role in production. Just as productive capital reduced the worker to the rank of an instrument which the capitalist uses in production, finance capital reduces the industrial and commercial capitalist to the status of a salaried employee of finance capital.

Alongside Finance Capital is Landowning Capital, which has ancient roots, but like Finance Capital plays no role in production. Finance capital is dealt with in Part IV and landowning capital in Part V of Volume Three.

Each of these three layers corresponds to a distinctive economic ethos. In bourgeois society, products are sold at their value. In productive capitalism, products are sold at the cost of production plus profit. Finance and landowning capital play no role in production and its property (credit or land) is loaned at interest, but never alienated.

The above formation represents developed *industrial capitalism*, now dominated by finance capital.

1.2 *The Logical Division of the Subject Matter*

Like the *Encyclopaedia*, (Logic, Nature and Spirit) the three Volumes of *Capital* form a syllogism.

1.2.1 The Immediate Production of Capital

Based on the foundation created with the definition of value in Part I, Volume One defines the unit of capital in Part II, and each is analysed as independent of every other unit. Each unit produces commodities each of whose value is composed of constant capital (the value of means of production consumed in production), variable capital (the value of the labour-power consumed) and surplus value (the product of unpaid labour-time).

The total value of each of these components corresponds to the same component part of the total social labour, which can be derived by simple addition because each unit of capital is considered separately side by side.

Commodities are sold at their value by each unit. Although competition between independent units and the independence of its units are essential to the nature of capitalism, Marx only touched on an analysis of competition at the end of Part II of Volume Three.

But the tendency of prices to their average does not affect the total value of each component, but only the division of value between buyer and seller. The division of the total social labour between constant, variable and surplus value is the secure outcome of Volume One. Nothing which follows in *Capital* or in real life undermines this conclusion.

A number of important tendencies are also established, such as the on-going revolution in technique with the resulting reduction in necessary labour time, the drive to increase the length of the working day, the dependence of profit on the length of the working day and the impoverishment of the working class.

1.2.2 The Circulation of Capital

Volume Two concerns the circulation of capital. Each of the separate capitals of Volume One are now analysed as connected in circuits of value beginning and ending with the sum of money-capital advanced for production. The value circuit begins from money-capital purchasing inputs, production itself, the sale of the commodities, and the return to money-capital in expanded form. This value circuit cannot on its own sustain conditions for the continued accumulation of capital and an on-going form of life. It is not enough that *value* must complete the circuit from money-capital through production to commodity-capital and conversion back into money-capital – each of the actual forms of labour and components of capital must be renewed.

The unit on which Volume Two is based is the circuit of a single capital, like the unit defined in Part II of Volume I, but now including the production process and the circulation of commodities within the unit. Each component part of the production process, including all the machinery and the raw materials and labour-power, must be renewed, as well as all the divers artefacts and activities which are realised as equivalents of the surplus labour appropriated in production, activities without which the capitalist social formation cannot exist.

This circuit, beginning and ending with money-capital, is the universal circuit of capital, and must be accompanied by particular circuits of capital – the circuit of commodity-capital (recovering a stock of commodities of all kinds, approximating in abundance the demand for each) and the circuit of productive-capital (the maintenance, repair and upgrading of machinery, acquisition of new supplies of raw material, and the needs of the workforce duly met ready for a new cycle of production).

In addition to these three units, the circuit of commodity-capital must be divided into the circuits corresponding to constant capital, the subsistence products for the life of the workers and the luxury consumer goods for the capitalists themselves.

Note that the two-layer logical division of the subject matter set out by the foregoing accords with Hegel's requirement in the *Logic* that each unit first be analysed on its own, before it is mediated through its relations with other units. Thus, the different capitals are still taken as if completing the circuit as independent units of capital, as if the renewal of all its components was the work of each unit of value acting separately.

1.2.3 The Process of Capitalist Production as a Whole

Volume Three concerns the process of capitalist production as a whole, the unity of production and circulation. The units of capital now no longer act side-by-side, independently of one another, but also act upon one another. The social capital is taken to be an integral whole, with each unit of capital acting upon others through the commodity market and the capital market.

Specifically, this means that the surplus value appropriated from unpaid labour by each of the capitals is shared amongst units of capital, whether or not they be productive, in proportion to the size of each capital. This sharing of surplus value effects the equalisation of the rate of profit on capital, and products are accordingly sold at cost-price plus profit, profit being calculated according to the general rate of profit.

Part III of Volume Three completes the conceptual reconstruction of industrial capital as such.

Volume Three continues the examination of the process whereby productive capitals share their surplus value to include the sharing of surplus value with finance capital and landowning capital. The schema used in the foregoing parts of *Capital*, in which first the total is determined before its division into parts, is repeated in the relation between productive capital and finance capital. No new surplus value is produced by finance capital and landowning capital.

Just as industrial capital arose on the basis of bourgeois society and subordinated bourgeois society to its own laws, finance capital arises from productive capital and subordinates productive capital to its own laws.

1.3 *Analysis by Units*

I have presented the major arcs of synthesis so that the reader may get an overall picture of the structure of the whole work before plunging into matters of detail. However, before it is possible to synthesise one must analyse. Just as each Book of Hegel's *Encyclopaedia* begins with a germ cell or unit, each Part of *Capital* identifies a novel unit and analyses it. A contradiction within the unit is identified and that contradiction is unfolded up to its limit. I say "novel" because each of these 15 units represents a unique insight into the structure of the concrete subject matter, with each successive unit arising out of the foregoing exposition. The identification of each of these units is a creative insight by Marx.

Once the entire field of phenomena is analysed into units, the synthesis (as outlined above) reconstructs the whole.

1.3.1 The Commodity (v.1 Part 1)

Capital begins with the commodity, the simplest social form of value, the economic cell-form. The commodity is the foundation of the whole work in the sense that the whole of *Capital* is concerned with the transformation and distribution of value in a series of different forms of value. The concept of "value" is thus concretised by the identification of these successive forms, each arising in given circumstances. A concrete concept of "value" necessarily entails connecting all of these forms together.

Each commodity is a particular kind of labour, use-value, and its magnitude, exchange value—is abstract labour-time, the socially average time required for the production of the given use-value. Exchange value is more fundamental than price, which is but the *appearance* of value, affected by a multiplicity of social conditions manifested only when the commodity is exchanged. The substance of value is therefore abstract labour-time, whatever the form of value.

The contradiction within the commodity is that the need of the user which is served by the use-value on one hand, and on the other hand, the seller's riches constituted by the exchange value, each belong to distinct processes. Whilst this contradiction provides the engine which Adam Smith identified as a great organising principle, 'self-interest', the two processes inevitably come into conflict and prove to be antagonistic.

1.3.2 The Embryo Capitalist, Moneybags (v.1 Part II)

The embryonic unit of capital is an individual capitalist who buys in order to sell more dearly. The individual capitalist develops into a capitalist firm. The universal form of capitalist firm is the industrial capitalist, which exists alongside the continued existence of the merchant capitalist and the usurer.

Capital is a unique form of value which can arise neither within circulation nor outside circulation, but must continuously be put into circulation and withdrawn again. The universal form of capital is industrial capital which employs labour-power and expands its magnitude by appropriation of surplus value from the labourer.

1.3.3 Unpaid Labour Time (v.1 Part III)

The surplus value acquired by an industrial capitalist through the employment of wage-labour is the unpaid labour-time worked every day by the labourer over and above the time necessary to produce the equivalent of their wage, their subsistence needs for the day. This surplus value is appropriated by forcing the labourer to work unpaid labour time. All the surplus value accrued by the total social capital and subsequently redistributed among the various sectors of the capitalist class, and subsequently shared with landowners and finance capitalists is equal to the total of unpaid labour time of all the workers involved in the cooperative production process.

In the same part of Volume One, Marx defines second order units which are the three component parts of capital: constant capital, variable capital and surplus value. Constant capital is the value of the productive capital which is merely transformed and reproduced with a constant magnitude of value in production.

Unpaid labour time is the bone of contention between the two classes, workers and capitalists.

1.3.4 The Necessary Labour Time (v.1 Part IV)

The necessary labour time is the time required by each worker, on average, to produce the equivalent of their daily needs. This is paid by the capitalist to the worker. Its significance is that the progressive development of the productive forces by productive capital tends to continuously reduce this necessary labour time, which constitutes the share of the total social labour which accrues to the working class.

In their endeavours to increase their profits by increasing the productivity of labour with the aim of increasing their profits, the capitalists collectively reduce the rate of profit by reducing the portion of capital which generates their profit.

1.3.5 Productive Labour (v.1 Part V)

Here Marx identifies the unit of productive labour. Unlike the capitalist who counted only the "hands-on" front line worker as "productive," Marx says that "it is no longer necessary for you to do manual work yourself; enough, if you are an organ of the collective labourer." On the other hand, there may be labour which the capitalist may rate as the most productive which in fact does not add to surplus value at all.

1.3.6 The Day's Wage (v.1 Part VI)

The industrial capitalist pays the day's wage to the worker for the use of their labour-power for an entire working day. Its value, however, is the necessary labour time. Marx isolates this unit to analyse the various particular forms of payment which serve to disguise the nature of the value of the worker's labour-power.

1.3.7 The Circuit of Capital (v.2 Part I)

The basic unit of Volume Two is the complete circuit of a commodity from the form of money-capital to productive capital to commodity-capital and back to money-capital, ready for reinvestment, but in expanded magnitude.

This *universal* unit is interlaced with the *particular* units being the circuit of commodity-capital and the circuit of productive capital.

Each individual capital plays a part in ensuring the conditions for the renewal of each circuit. Through crises and accidents the multitude of blockages must be overcome in the absence of any overall plan.

1.3.8 The Turnover Time of Capital (v.2 Part II)

Turnover is the time taken for a unit of capital to complete its circuit and return to capital in the same form. The turnover time makes the denominator in determination of the rate of profit.

The need to put capital into circulation and pull it back out as fast as possible forces the capitalist to try to reduce the turnover time.

1.3.9 The Unity of Circulation and Production (v.2 Part III)

This circuit is the process by means of which a unit of capital circulates so as to reproduce the *entire* capitalist social formation, and not confined to the circuit of productive capital, and functions as the unit which is generalised here to include the reproduction of all facets of the capitalist social formation.

Capital must not only renew itself, but must renew the entire social formation.

1.3.10 Cost-price and Price of Production (v.3 Part I)

The cost-price of production is the portion of the total value of a commodity which is accounted for by the total capital invested, irrespective of its division into constant capital and wages. The price of production is the cost-price plus profit on the total capital invested.

Cost-price and price of production are both mere appearances and do not correspond to objective needs of society for its reproduction. This is the *appearance* of the economic categories under the rule of capital.

1.3.11 The Average Rate of Profit (v.3 Part II)

The average rate of profit is the total social surplus divided by the total capital invested in a given period of time, such as a year. This rate is generalised by the joint action of the commodity market and the capital market and applies to all units of capital whether productive or commercial.

The rate of profit can be equalised only by industries which are inherently more profitable cross-subsidising those sectors which have a large quota of constant capital to sustain. This happens by commodities being sold above or below their value and by the movement of capital on the capital market.

1.3.12 Accumulated Constant Capital (v.3 Part III)

Marx demonstrates that the drive to increase the productivity of labour inevitably leads to a disproportionate increase in the mass of material and machinery which the capitalist has accumulated and which must be engaged in production. Therefore, with the increase in the rate of surplus value, the absolute value of profit grows, but its proportion to capital advanced, the rate of profit, tends to decline. Here the fundamental contradiction between production for profit and production for human needs is manifested.

1.3.13 The Commercial Capitalist (v.3 Part IV)

The commercial capitalist is a capitalist firm which buys in order to sell more dearly, but deals solely with forms of credit arising in the circuit of commodity capital.

The activity of commercial capital in its pure form is speculative and does not contribute to creation of the social surplus at all.

1.3.14 The Finance Capitalist (v.3 Part V)

The finance capitalist is a capitalist firm which *loans* money-capital without releasing ownership of it, and charges interest for use of the money-capital. This is the universal form of finance capital; particular forms of finance capital include those firms who hire out the use of infrastructure such as warehouses or roads or platforms like Facebook or Google Earth on the same basis.

In finance capital function is divorced from ownership. The interest of finance capital in the expansion of credit serves only as a burden on the back of productive capital and the source of a new class antagonism.

1.3.15 The Landowner (v.3 Part VI)

The private landowner is a unit which plays no part in production whatsoever, but charges a levy on productive capital by means of its monopoly control of land.

The private landowner is a redundant class, surviving only on the basis of an inherited monopoly of the land.

2 Marx's *Capital*: Outstanding Issues

Marx made a more or less complete conceptual reconstruction of capital as it had developed in Britain in the late 19th century. There are elements of this reconstruction which were not completed, generally because at the time they had not shown themselves to be the site of significant issues for the development of the capitalist economy, the class struggle or ideology. There are also processes which lie outside what Marx took to be the scope of his conceptual reconstruction which have become significant for the economy itself.

Among those processes which are part of the economic system but which require further analysis are: (1) Commodities, (2) Precarity and gig work, (3) State intervention, (4) the advertising industry, and (5) The international development of capital.

In addition there are processes which exist independently of the economic structure but which interact with the economy to a significant degree: (1) the labour process in general, especially the development of technology – especially AI, the internet and "the internet of things" and automated social control in particular, (2) the organised workers' movement and its place in society, (3) the women's movement and the social position of women in general, (4) the international configuration of capital, and (5) anthropogenic climate change. It would be out of place to deal with these latter questions, but it is these processes which have had the most profound impact on life under capitalism, while not, in my view, warranting any revision of the analysis of capitalism given in *Capital*. However, this is a book about *Capital* and I will defer these issues to another day.

2.1 *Commodities*

Marx has analysed the commodity in terms of the use value and exchange value of social labour. This remains the foundation of any analysis of the commodity. However, the form of the commodity has changed a great deal since the heyday of industrial capitalism.

Marx has already commented on the transport industry:

> what the transportation industry sells is change of location. The useful effect is inseparably connected with the process of transportation, i.e., the productive process of the transport industry. ... The useful effect can be consumed only during this process of production. It does not exist as a utility different from this process, a use-thing which does not function as an article of commerce, does not circulate as a commodity, until after it has been produced. But the exchange-value of this useful effect is determined, like that of any other commodity
>
> MARX, 1894, Chapter 1

The railway industry was at its peak in America from 1870 to 1917, and was a key component of the expansion of industry in the US. The railway industry was in no sense peripheral to capitalist development and Marx would have been keenly observing this. These comments apply equally well to any service industry.

In Marx's day, *service industries* were almost exclusively to be found in the domestic consumption of surplus value by the capitalists, and he did not dwell on services as a form of commodity. The more so because the conception of wage-labour as a service alongside rent of land or investment of capital was a rival theory of political economy. (See Chapter 21 of *Theories of Surplus Value*). Domestic servants, lawyers and so on, he did not see as productive workers, but on the other hand:

> a schoolmaster is a productive labourer when, in addition to belabouring the heads of his scholars, he works like a horse to enrich the school proprietor.
>
> MARX, 1867, Chapter 16

And Marx notes that renting out warehouses or collecting tolls on private roads is to be taken as a species of finance capital. In relation to finance capital proper, Marx says:

> loaning money for a certain time and receiving it back with interest (surplus-value) is the complete form of the movement peculiar to interest-bearing capital as such. … A special sort of commodity, capital has its own peculiar mode of alienation.
>
> MARX, 1894, Chapter 21

Money loaned for use as capital he called the capital-commodity. Marx correctly saw industrial capitalism as the universal instance of capitalism the analysis of which would therefore generate the principles which could be extended with appropriate modification to other particular forms of capitalist enterprise. This was the situation with the transport and education industries and with even more modification to finance capital.

Marx has nothing to say in *Capital* about intellectual property, but there is no reason to think he did not recognise it. But the idea that intellectual property could be produced by corporations using industrial methods of production, and distributing it without any transmission of matter (as is the case today) was surely beyond anyone's imagination at the time. However, the economic status of a MicroSoft application is surely no different than that of a warehouse or toll road. But a MicroSoft application is an industrial commodity not a financial service. It requires considerable labour time to produce, maintain and upgrade just like a factory. Its peculiarity is that it can be replicated like a book or work of art. But unauthorised copying and distribution of computer code is theft, just as it is for literature and artworks. Likewise, a platform like Facebook is in principle little different from a tollway or storage unit which is enhanced by nearby development, except that ownership is not functionally separated from production. The phenomenon in which corporations appropriate the unpaid labour of users of their platform also poses novel economic problems.

However, the fact that the economic relations entailed in the production, maintenance, distribution and use of computer code is the same as that in the case of an industrial commodity, does not take away from the profound impact this kind of product has on both the labour process and everyday life and consequently on ideology and politics.

Services, whether professional services like legal or medical services, industrial services, like transport, maintenance, waste disposal, etc., or consulting services, marketing and other services to capital, are forms of commodity, though not *necessarily* thereby *productive*. Again, however, this kind of work entails enormous changes in the labour process and everyday life and consequent changes in the *Zeitgeist*.

Services cannot be accumulated as industrial commodities can. But accumulation of commodities is a fruitless and unproductive activity in any case. It remains only money which can be accumulated and constitute a form of capital, and then is not capital but a hoard unless it is repeatedly put back into circulation. And in this respect, services and intellectual property function perfectly well as a form of wealth and capital.

2.2 *Precarity and Gig Work*

Part-time, casual and piece work have been around for as long as capitalism. Marx insisted that the definitive, universal form of work was the provision of labour-power to be applied under the direction of the capitalist for the entire working day, the duration of which was generally fixed by law in a given community, though the subject of industrial struggle. In this context, other forms of labour, such as piece work and casual labour, were used by capitalists as a means of intensifying and disciplining labour. These were taken as day-labour by other means.

Subsequently, the norm in developed capitalist countries became labour under a contract which generally guaranteed employment for a more extended period. Again, this would be theorised on the basis of the same principles, in this case modified somewhat to the benefit of the worker, as compared to the day-labour which formed the model for Marx's conception of wage-labour.

When the post-war boom busted and the world was plunged into stagflation, part-time and casual work made a resurgence which continues to this day. It must be observed though that this practice results in a self-inflicted limitation on the amount of labour-power available for use by a capitalist per working day. This creates what Marx called "the reserve army of labour." In other words, capitalists have collectively decided to employ *less* labour-power in order to maintain the *precarity* of their employees. Precarity now is the dominant condition for a significant section of the working class, making any settled form of family life out of reach for many.

Likewise, compelling workers to constitute themselves as a legal company and offer their labour for sale on the market has the effect of imposing precarity as well as burdening the workers with all the bureaucracy and expense of the pretence of running a "business." Evidently, this serves the same end as promoting precarity. Perversely though, making workers identify and live as "contractors" can have the ideological effect of them identifying as "small businesspeople" while in terms of material conditions they have been thrown into the lowest ranks of the proletariat.

Work from home has been added to the variety of modes of employment since the COVID pandemic, relieving employers of much of the burdens of supervision and placing responsibility for the workplace on to the worker and increasing the flexibility of work to the maximum.

Gig work concentrates all of these forms of intensifying labour in a single technique, intensifying precarity to the maximum, with part-time and casual working, piece work, work-from-home and outsourcing combined. While social media technology enables gig work, there is no technical reason the benefits of the technology to clients cannot be used in the context of secure employment contracts. All of these forms of intensification of labour aggravate the difficulties of workers' organisation.

This difficulty confronting organized labour comes via all these types of irregular working which are connected to the postmodern ethos, giving material expression to the fluid nature of reality characteristic of postmodern thinking. This is complicated by the fact that some workers *prefer* aspects of these modes of work, particularly professional workers.

Nonetheless, during the period when *Capital* was published, dockworkers waited outside the gates while supervisors threw brass tokens into the crowd which were to be presented to apply for one day's work, and the General Council of the International Workingmen's Association included a journalist, two shoemakers and a watchmaker all of whom belonged to their trade union but worked in conditions more akin to today's professionals and small businesspeople. So these precarious forms of labour are not entirely novel, but in the wake of the long postwar boom when the labour movement was strong, they have made a resurgence.

From a social and ideological point of view, these changes in the form of wages are profound but from the point of view of economics they are still wages.

2.3 *The Advertising Industry*

On the surface, advertising and marketing are developments promoting the circulation of commodities and the realisation of the value of commodity-capital. But they are entirely parasitic on the circulation of commodities, serving to monetise commodity-capital, mainly by the generation of new desires whose contribution to human culture is suspect to say the least.

But more importantly, they provide the means of monetising all sorts of activities, particularly in the entertainment industry which has now burgeoned to become one of the largest industries in a postmodern capitalist economy. Advertising and all kinds of work, broadly in the entertainment industry plays a problematic role in the circulation of capital. Advertising is the fuel which powers the internet, and the internet in turn is now a crucial element of all aspects of social life.

2.4 *State Intervention*

According to Geert Reuten (2019) the state budget in the core OECD countries has increased from about 11% in 1870 to about 45% of GDP today. The overwhelming majority of that 45% is transfers, mostly to pensioners of various kinds, and in addition to these transfers, public health and education, public transport and communication infrastructure and other public endeavours on the part of all levels of government, paid for generally out of tax revenue, constitute a huge stabilising portion of the capitalist economy alongside defence, border security and other activities of government.

The period of neo-liberalism, broadly from the election of Thatcher and Reagan in 1979 till the Economic crisis of 2008, has lingered on for a couple of decades, but in the wake of the COVID pandemic, the state is now the first port of call in a crisis, while social democrats and right-wing populists alike rely on state enterprises for key economic policy initiatives.

Any updating of *Capital* will have to encompass state enterprises and state intervention in the economy as key elements of the capitalist economy. As I wrote in the companion to this work, the state and the economy cannot be conceptualised as an original unity. Each is the product of a different process and the two processes intersect in government enterprises. Nevertheless, the state can generally be relied upon to do whatever is necessary to sustain capitalist development, with or without revolutionary socialists in the government. As Reuten observed, the state was only just able to head off a domino-effect collapse of the world economy in 2009 by, for example, nationalising the US car industry for a period of time.

As Marx observed in Part V of Volume Three of *Capital*, finance capital arises at first from the business of the circulation of commodity-capital and then displaces productive capital, reducing former industrial capitalists to the status of salaried employees. Nothing more than the nationalisation of finance capital would be required to create a form of state-capitalism or Socialism, depending on whether the state genuinely reflected the will of the people.

But laying utopian visions to the side, the conflict between human flourishing and the capitalist mode of production expressed in the private ownership of all kinds of essential postmodern infrastructure is an open sore. But what kind of social control would a democratic form of state exercise over this infrastructure which would make any real difference to how they work? Would gig work be any the less exploitative? Would social media be any the less destructive of human sociality?

The investigation of such questions goes way beyond the scope of political economy, but at the same time poses new problems for political economy. In my view, the question posed is not state control of the economy, but how the withering away of the state can accompany the problems which have generated a renewed turn to the capitalist state as the manager of the capitalist economy. But finance capital remains the great stumbling block to any progress towards Socialism of any kind. Its abolition cannot be bypassed.

2.5 *Summary*

In summary, I believe all the above issues are worthy of research and indeed are already the subject of research. But none of these issues, in my view, undermines the status of *Capital* as the definitive foundation for the political economics of capitalism or warrant the declaration of a "new mode of production."

The outstanding and unresolved questions are chiefly those posed by the politics and ideology of a society created by the labour process to which capitalism has given birth: on one hand, gig work from home by outsourced workers paid by piece work, whether delivery drivers or scientific consultants. On the other hand, finance capital owning and controlling the majority of capital beyond the control of governments and people, while making no contribution to production.

The contradiction between the mode of production and the forces of production is at a critical point. Capital is ripe for socialisation if only a democratic form of social life capable of using these forces of production could be built.

3 Reflection

3.1 *The* Capital/Logic *Debate*

How was it that Russian Marxists had recognised the Hegelian structure of *Capital* 90 years ago, and yet the flurry of investigations into the relation between the *Logic* and *Capital* since the publication of the *Grundrisse* in the West in 1973 failed to identify this structure?

Well, Lenin, who alerted us to this relation back in 1915 may have misled us by telling us to focus on the first chapter. Undue focus on the first chapter in which both the *Logic* and *Capital* are concerned with Measure may have misled people. The *Grundrisse* which seems to follow the *Logic* somewhat mechanically may have gained attention for the issue, but also misled people who never looked for the structural relation between *Logic* and *Capital*. And Marx himself didn't help by never making explicit his debt to Hegel.

The Soviet Marxists who have been my teachers in this matter have remained largely unknown outside the disciplines of child development and education. Their work was suppressed in the USSR, so it was unknown to members of the Communist parties around the world, and by the latter part of the twentieth century when their works became available in the West, academia had turned its back on Soviet Marxism.

Still, why is it that this relationship between *Capital* and the *Logic* was not picked up independently by academics in the West? It seems to me that the fundamental problem here is the silo structure of academia. All the participants in this debate have been Marxists. Hegel scholars have largely dismissed Marx as having misunderstood and distorted Hegel and confine themselves to the world of early 19th century German philosophy. The only exception to this whom I have found is Richard Winfield, an excellent Hegel scholar who also identifies as a Marxist. The Marxists on the other hand, while intimately familiar with Marx's economic manuscripts in almost every case have only the most superficial and/or secondhand knowledge of Hegel. Chris Arthur certainly has studied the *Logic*, but somehow, Arthur failed to see the wood for the trees in his focus on the early chapters of *Capital*. In any case, there was no one who had a real scholarly knowledge of both Hegel and Marx. Hegel and Marx belonged to different departments of the academy and no one could put the two together.

Likewise, it seems that Economics and Philosophy belong to different academic departments, and the one writer I studied who exhibited a real knowledge of capitalist economics, Geert Reuten, made a mess of the philosophical basis of Marx's *Capital*.

So it turned out that I was in a unique position of having a relatively close familiarity with both *Capital* and the *Logic*. This was possible because I did not learn my Marx or my Hegel in the academy, but mostly by private study as an autodidact. So it was that I was the first to see the several layers of symmetry between the structure of the two works. On the other hand, I am an autodidact, and it remains the case that academia instils a discipline in writers which is difficult for the autodidact to attain independently. However, if the academics take my contribution seriously, perhaps they can take my insights further thanks to their specialist knowledge. That is my hope.

3.2 *My Journey to* Capital

I first read *Capital* in 1972 during a period of quiet reflection while living with my partner and two children on common land in the North of England. On reflection, I don't think I got further than Part III of Volume Three. At that point in my life I had never joined a Marxist group, and I formed my own interpretation of *Capital* on the basis independent study of Marx's classic works and a very slim knowledge of economics, particularly the impending crisis of stagflation hitting the capitalist world at this time.

After returning to London, I joined the WRP and here I had the benefit of talks on Marxist economics from Geoff Pilling. Until the 1980s then I had a more or less conventional understanding of *Capital*, but unlike some people today, I never saw *Capital* as an ahistorical work of Logic.

While still a member of the WRP I was exposed to the study of Lenin's *Annotations on Hegel's Science of Logic* and acquired my own copies of the *Science of Logic* and the *Encyclopaedic Logic*. I continued to work with Hegel's *Logic* after returning to Australia in 1985 up to the present time. The WRP was also responsible for introducing me to the Soviet philosopher E.V. Ilyenkov.

Ilyenkov's *The Abstract and Concrete in Marx's Capital* (1960) had a strong influence on me and shaped my reading of *Capital* until about 2020.

In the late 1990s, three important turns came in my life.

(1) Having failed to get a Hegel reading group going with others on the Left in Melbourne, I launched the website Hegel-by-HyperText. Copy typing screeds of Hegel into web pages created a "honey pot" which attracted people interested in Hegel studies from across the world and I was able to learn from email discussions with a variety of others with varying levels of understanding Hegel. The website grew to become a more or less comprehensive archive of Hegel's most important works as scanners and OCR accelerated the work of building the archive. This led to my becoming much more familiar with Hegel's work which culminated in 2019 with my publication of *Hegel for Social Movements*. This book presented a reading of Hegel which made Hegel relevant to present-day social issues and accessible to people beyond the University philosophy departments.

(2) I joined the Marxists Internet Archive and took on the task of administering the Reference Archive and the Marx-Engels Archive. Again, this engaged me in a lot of low-skill work with Marx's texts, but also opened me to discussions with every kind of Marxist in the world as people interacted with us for a variety of reasons. This gave me a great deal of familiarity with the breadth of Marx and Engels' work and the variety of opinions about it outside my own circle. But, to be honest, my knowledge of *Capital* and Marx's work generally was still superficial.

(3) I joined the listserv XMCA devoted to the study of the Cultural Psychology of Lev Vygotsky and the Soviet Activity Theorists. This discourse became my intellectual home. I had become very tired of all of the varieties of orthodox Marxism, but in CHAT (Cultural-Historical Activity Theory) I discovered a strain of Marxism which was deeply embedded in disciplines like Early Childhood Development and Education and had more or less abstained from political disputation throughout the twentieth century. This feature had been more or less a survival strategy in Stalin's USSR and then in the USA. But it was not a "political line" I was looking for. Here I found a current of Marxism which had survived the distortions and atrocities of "the Party line," and renewed my interest in Vygotsky, A.N. Leontyev and Ilyenkov.

From Vygotsky and the Activity Theorists I learnt the method of the "germ cell," which Vygotsky had developed and used to revolutionise five different branches of Psychology. Vygotsky had not read Hegel (except possibly for the section of the *Subjective Spirit* on "Psychology"), but he had read *Capital* very closely and it was Vygotsky who first (so far as I know) recognised that Marx was using the commodity as a "germ cell." I used this observation in all my writing on Vygotsky and Activity Theory from my first published book in 2009 onwards.

However, by the time I got to write *Hegel for Social Movements* in 2019 I had still not found *where* in the *Logic* Hegel had *explained* this method, notwithstanding that I could see with my own eyes that he applied it throughout the *Encyclopaedia*. After sending off to the publisher the proofs of *Hegel for Social Movements*, and freeing my mind to move on, I set about solving this puzzle. I reached out to Paul Redding and together we thought of German words which could mean something like "unit" and we came up with *Einzelheit*. And there it was, under the heading of "Division" in "The Idea of the True" in the second last chapter of the *Science of Logic*, though absent from the *Shorter Logic*. Suddenly, my reading of Hegel had been transformed. Looking back at the *Encyclopaedia*, I could *see* how Hegel applied the "germ cell" method to more than 30 sciences.

Now I turned to *Capital*, and I could see that Marx used the germ cell method not just with the commodity, but *repeatedly*. In a talk at International Friends of Ilyenkov Conference, in London in November 2022, I presented a paper which claimed that Marx had proposed a germ cell at "numerous" point in *Capital*. This thesis was rejected by those attending the Conference. Ilyenkov had already said that the commodity was the germ cell of capitalism and that was that.

In 2023, I wrote the first version of this book as a PDF on my web page. I shared this with Tony Smith, who with Fred Moseley had edited the volume "Marx's *Capital* and Hegel's *Logic*" which was the stimulus for my writing on this topic. Tony gave me fulsome praise for trying, but tore strips off my article. He was right. I needed to read the existing literature much more seriously and I needed to study *Capital* more thoroughly before I could pretend to speak on this topic.

As a result I sat down to read through the literature on the *Capital/Logic* debate. I learnt a great deal about Marx's work on political economy from this study. I came to realise how superficial my knowledge of Marx and *Capital* really was. Nevertheless, I was able to write the companion volume, refuting in detail all the books and articles which have been written on this topic by recent authors. And given that I had not discovered "The Idea of the True" till almost 40 years after I first read *The Science of Logic*, I could not blame others for failing to find it. But, in my own defence, I had noticed this feature of the structure of the *Encyclopaedia* long ago, I just hadn't yet discovered where Hegel *explained* this method till 2020. I doubt that any of the writers in this discourse had bothered to read the *Encyclopaedia.*

So once having sent the manuscript off to the publisher before Christmas 2024 I settled down to read the three volumes of *Capital* from beginning to end, and identify all of the germ cells I could find. I discovered then that Marx's division of *Capital* into parts followed the development of germ cells, just as Hegel had structured the divisions of the *Encyclopaedia* in the same way. There was a germ cell for 15 of the 18 Parts of *Capital.* The remaining three parts covered historical or miscellaneous topics.

While I had become very familiar with Volume One of *Capital* over the years, the second and third volumes were largely terra incognito for me up till this time. So, I was delighted to find the germ cell structure continued right to the end. But I also studied for the first time (so far as I can remember) Marx's remarks about finance capital. I immediately recognised this as a new, third ethical order. It also solved the problem Marx had had with the notion of an "individual capital." It was only then, just before receiving back the proofs of the first volume from the publisher that I recalled that this idea of three different moral orders overlaying and conflicting with one another was found in the structure of Hegel's *Philosophy of Right* as well!

53 years after first reading *Capital* I was still discovering new layers of Hegelian structure in *Capital*!

4 Conclusion

Lev Vygotsky left us five examples of the germ cell method in Psychology, and Activity Theorists since then have applied the approach in a number of fields of research. Marx left us fifteen examples in *Capital.* So we have plenty of exemplary works to show how this method can be applied to the solution of complex problems.

Marx and Hegel each left exemplars of how multiple ethical realms coexist in modern society helping to make sense of how we live in complex social formations. And Hegel's Logic, the logic of practice, was exhaustively outlined in his own Idealist style in the *Science of Logic.* My aim with this work was to highlight the use of these paradigmatic works in a study of Marx's *Capital.*

The hope, implied in *Capital* and embraced by many generations of Socialists, that the "expropriators will be expropriated" and control of the forces of production fall into the hands of the popular masses, fails to convince anyone today. When Marxists seized power in the USSR in 1917, the state which resulted turned out to be both oppressive and obsolete. While universal suffrage prevails in most of the world, no country has elected a government which has done any more than manage capitalism and bring closer the collapse of the natural conditions for human life. Why on Earth would anyone believe that a world economy which fell into the hands of governments elected by universal suffrage would do anything better than the billionaires? And yet, how could we expect a people which was incapable of making rational collective decisions at almost any level to do better when blessed with the right of universal suffrage?

To rein in the postmodern forces of production created by capitalism poses a huge development of the cognitive and organizing capacity of human beings en masse. Learning to develop and exercise our common will *despite capitalism* needs to begin with much more modest tasks than the implementation of Socialism. The only thing I can say for certain is that there is no place in the coming revolution for a "revolutionary party." Parties belong to the modern era. *Every* social layer will have to participate in the change to come.

References

Arthur, C. (2011). *Towards a Systematic Dialectic of Capital.* https://chrisarthur.net.

Blunden, A. (2024). *The Capital / Logic Debate.* Leiden, NL: Brill.

Blunden, A. (2016). *The Origins of Collective Decision Making.* Leiden, NL: Brill.

Brenkert, G. (1983). *Marx's Ethic of Freedom.* Routledge & Kegan Paul.

Fraser, N. & Gordon, L. (1990). *A Genealogy of Dependency: Tracing a keyword of the U.S. welfare state.* Chicago, IL: University of Chicago Press.

Hegel, G.W.F. (1969/1816). *Science of Logic.* "Book Three, Chapter 2, The Idea of Cognition," translated by A. V. Miller, George Allen & Unwin.

Hegel, G.W.F. (1952/1821). Hegel's *Philosophy of Right.* Tr. T.M. Knox. Oxford, UK: Clarendon Press.

Kautsky, K. (1892). *The Class Struggle.* (*The Erfurt Program*).

Laibman, D. (1993). Review: The Falling Rate of Profit: A New Empirical Study, pp. 223–233, *Science & Society*, 57(2), Sage.

Marx, K. (1844). *A Contribution to the Critique of Hegel's Philosophy of Right*, Introduction. Progress Publishers, USSR.

Marx, K. (1863). *Theories of Surplus Value*, "[Chapter X] Ricardo's and Adam Smith's Theory of Cost-price (Refutation)." Progress Publishers, USSR.

Marx, K. (1956/1867). *Capital Volume One. The Process of Production of Capital*, Progress Publishers, USSR.

Marx, K. (1959/1885). *Capital Volume Two. The Process of Circulation of Capital*, Progress Publishers, USSR.

Marx, K. (1959/1894). *Capital Volume Three. The Process of Capitalist Production as a Whole*, International Publishers, USSR.

Marx, K. (1973/1857). *The Grundrisse.* Tr Martin Nicolaus. Penguin.

Marx, K. (1994/1864). The Direct Process of Production, *MECW v. 34*. New York, NY: International Publishers.

Mark, K. (1989/1881). Notes on Adolph Wagner's "Lehrbuch der politischen Ökonomie." *MECW, v. 24*, p. 531. New York, NY: International Publishers.

Moseley, F. (1991). *The Falling Rate of Profit in the Postwar United States Economy.* Palgrave Macmillan.

Moseley, F. (2016). *Money and Totality. A Macro-Monetary Interpretation of Marx's Logic in* Capital *and the End of the 'Transformation Problem'.* Leiden, NL: Brill.

Reuten, G. (2019). *The Unity of the Capitalist Economy and State.* Brill. https://www.researchgate.net/publication/330152819.

Ricardo, D. (1817). *Principles of Political Economy and Taxation.*

Smith, A. (1776). *The Wealth of Nations.*

Taylor, F. (1991). *The Principles of Scientific Management.* Harper & Row.

Index

www.ingramcontent.com/pod-product-compliance
Lightning Source LLC
LaVergne TN
LVHW012259240826
846436LV00029B/394
9798888908914